J OSCELINE

C000220878

COOKING
FOR
CHRISTMAS

JOSCELINE DIMBLEBY

COOKING FOR CHRISTMAS

HOW TO PLAN, SURVIVE AND ENJOY CHRISTMAS

CLEARVIEW BOOKS

CLEARVIEW

CLEARVIEW

This edition published in the UK in 2015 by
Clearview Books, 22 Clarendon Gardens,
London W9 1AZ

Text copyright © Josceline Dimbleby 2015

First published 1978, revised edition published 1987

All rights reserved worldwide. No part of the
book may be copied or changed in any format,
sold, or used in a way other than what is outlined
in this book, under any circumstances.

A CIP catalogue record for this book is available from the
British Library

ISBN 978-1908337-207

Book design by Simonne Waud
Cover design by Jojo Hastie Design and Simonne Waud

Printed in the UK by Bell & Bain Ltd., Glasgow

CONTENTS

INTRODUCTION

In 1978 Sainsbury's decided they should start to publish small cookery books to be sold at the check out and asked me to write the first one. As the book would come out in late autumn, the run up to Christmas, and realising that no book on Christmas cooking existed at that time, I suggested *Cooking For Christmas*. I married into a large clan and had already been 'doing' Christmas for ten years. By then I had learnt how to cope with those few days that can seem as intense and complex as a military operation, and found ways to make them the most unifying moments of the year. I had discovered that planning and cooking ahead is the key to avoiding panic and stress, that you must give yourself time to think about the food, that even dishes you repeat each year can be given a new twist to make them even better. So I was glad of the opportunity to spread the word about my variations on a theme. Christmas is a time of heightened emotions that you can channel into your cooking; I believe the best dishes are made with love and that Christmas is an opportunity to make your family

and friends feel your love for them, and exclaim that the feast is even more delicious than ever this year.

By 1978 I had written two cookery books of original recipes, much inspired by my travelling childhood. My three children, sometimes unwillingly, were urged to try all sorts of unusual tastes, combinations and textures. But for my family Christmas I wanted to stick to traditional dishes, adding little ideas of my own, and above all good flavour. My own childhood Christmases in far-flung places had been far from traditional; my parents divorced when I was four years old and my mother married a diplomat who moved from post to post abroad. Since then my dream had always been of a close family Christmas that came round reassuringly every year in the same place with familiar rituals and food. At last marriage and children gave me the opportunity to create the kind of home and Christmas I had dreamed of, to be repeated for decades.

For the festive meal itself our family alternated between goose and turkey, though as soon as the children could influence decisions it had to be turkey. However, the blandest bird can be transformed by an interesting stuffing, full of contrasting flavours and textures. Each year I look back at this book and remember so much - not only the individual dishes but how people looked, what decorations I put on the table, even our conversations and laughter. Although I repeatedly say that I find it impossible to make the same dish twice Christmas is one occasion when I do - almost. There were many editions of *Cooking For Christmas* and each time I would make little changes or additions. My Christmas pudding became flourless and sugar free with added squidgy prunes for dark sweetness and fresh orange peel for a tang. The recipe that has made the greatest, most lasting impact is my Mince Pies with Orange Pastry; every Christmas to this day people say they are making them yet again. Now I tell them to mix a few raw cranberries in with the mincemeat as they form bright scarlet explosions as the pies cook, and add sharpness to the sweetness.

Cooking For Christmas is not just the Christmas meal, it is for the whole period surrounding it too. I hoped it would be like looking in on our family's Christmas, even being part of it; only recently I realised that many of my readers felt that it was their family life that I was part of. When I finally branched out into books not specifically about food and began talking at literary festivals all over the country, I met many people who had used my cookery books for decades. It was a wonderful experience; at every event several members of the audience would bring tattered and stained copies of my old cookery books for me to sign, above all *Cooking For Christmas*, telling me that they still used the book every year. On two separate occasions, when the audience were asking questions at the end of my talk a woman got up and told me that she felt I had been part of their family from one generation into another, and burst into tears. If that isn't an example of the extraordinary power of good food and the best possible reason to have written my books, what is?

Josceline Dimbleby

7

THE CHRISTMAS DINNER

I feel it's a mistake to think that the special atmosphere of Christmas Day will make this "meal of the year" taste good even if you make very little effort with the real flavour of the food. You must try and make it the best turkey they've ever tasted, with the most succulent stuffings, crisp fresh vegetables, golden crunchy potatoes and not a packet sauce in sight. (Well, if you must use packet bread sauce add more cloves, nutmeg and finely grated onion to it to give it zest!) Your Christmas pudding will be far more moist and crumbly if you make it yourself and you can buy packs of little silver charms to put in the mixture. It's all rather a lot of work, but how can a good Christmas not be – at least a lot of the cooking can be done well in advance and gives me, at any rate, a childish feeling of excited anticipation. More than any other meal, the Christmas dinner has to be planned step by step if you are going to remain calm: however disorganised a person you may be, you surely must write out a true plan of campaign for Christmas morning. This way you will have a much better chance of a relaxed and happy Christmas, leaving everyone with tantalising memories of your spectacular food.

ROAST TURKEY

Prepare your turkey for roasting the day before. Stuff each end of the bird* and rub lavishly all over with at least ¼ lb butter or margarine. Wrap up in well buttered foil and put in a roasting tin. On Christmas Day preheat the oven to Gas Mark 3/325°F/160°C (unless you are doing your roast potatoes in advance – see p.16). Put the turkey low down in the oven and cook for 2½–3 hours for a 6–8 lb (2.5–3.5 kg) bird, 3–3¾ hours for an 8–14 lb (3.5–6.0 kg) bird and 3¾-4¼ hours for a 14–18 lb (6.0–8.0 kg) bird. Three-quarters of an hour before it is ready, unwrap the foil to expose the turkey so that it will brown, and pour a glass of dry vermouth or white wine over it.

After you have transferred the turkey to a carving board make the gravy. Blend 1 rounded teaspoon (2 x 5 ml spoon) of arrowroot or cornflour with a little water and stir into the pan juices. Let this bubble over the heat until thickened and season to taste. Serve the gravy with the turkey, accompanied by cranberry sauce and bread sauce.

*Although many people do stuff both ends of the turkey, overfilling can result in the bird not being thoroughly cooked. Great care should be taken not to put too much stuffing in the body cavity, or the stuffing can be cooked separately and an onion or lemon placed in the bird during cooking.

STUFFINGS

Although the appearance of the golden turkey is exciting, the taste is often dull. However, if you take the trouble to make two excellent, contrasting stuffings the flavour will be infinitely superior. The Veal, Lemon and Parsley Stuffing should be used to stuff the neck cavity, while the Chestnut Stuffing may be cooked in a baking dish and served separately, or cooked in the body cavity.

CHESTNUT STUFFING

4 oz (100 g) smoked streaky bacon
2 oz (50 g) butter
1 onion – peeled and chopped finely
turkey heart and liver – chopped finely
6 oz (150 g) sliced mushrooms
10 oz (250 g) chestnut purée
1 small tin or tube of liver pâté
3 large cloves garlic – chopped finely
1 tablespoon (15 ml spoon) dried
*   oregano*
2 oz (50 g) fresh breadcrumbs
1 lightly whisked egg
salt, black pepper

Cut the rind off the bacon and chop into small cubes. Put the butter in a pan and fry the bacon, the onion and the turkey heart and liver for 3–5 minutes. Transfer to a bowl with all the fat, stir in all the other ingredients thoroughly with a wooden spoon and season well. Fill baking dish, baste with a little of the turkey juices and place in the oven to cook with the bird for the final ¾ hour.

SPECIAL CHESTNUT AND PARSNIP STUFFING FOR TURKEY OR GOOSE
Serves 8–10

This is the least stodgy stuffing I know: sweet, aromatic, almost a dish on its own. Dried mushrooms are expensive and not strictly necessary, but they do add to the flavour.

¾ oz (20 g) packet of dried mushrooms
¼ pint (150 ml) hot water
1½-inch (4 cm) piece of fresh ginger
4 garlic cloves
2 oz (50 g) dried apricots
12 oz (375 g) parsnips
2 oz (50 g) butter
1 tablespoon (15 ml spoon) olive oil
15 oz (475 g) can of whole peeled
*   chestnuts*
2 oz (50 g) walnuts, chopped roughly
salt, black pepper

First put the dried mushrooms in a bowl with the hot water and soak for 2 hours or so. Then peel the ginger and garlic and chop them together finely. Chop the dried apricots fairly small. Peel the parsnips and chop them into small pieces.

Melt the butter with the olive oil over a medium heat in a large frying-pan. Add the parsnips and stir them around for 8–12 minutes until they are almost soft. Add the ginger and the garlic and stir for a minute. Increase the heat to high, add the chopped apricots and the mushrooms and their soaking liquid and allow to bubble, without stirring, for about 2 minutes until the liquid has been almost completely absorbed. Turn into a mixing bowl. Drain the chestnuts and cut them up roughly. Add them to the stuffing mixture, with the chopped walnuts, and mix gently together with a wooden spoon, seasoning generously with salt and a little black pepper.

GREEN STUFFING
Serves 8–10

This can be a second stuffing for one end of the turkey, but it is also excellent on its own if you feel like something less rich than usual.

1 lb (500 g) thin leeks
8 oz (250 g) spring greens
2 large garlic cloves
a large bunch of parsley
4 oz (125 g) butter
1 tablespoon (15 ml spoon) chopped
  tarragon
2 teaspoons (2 x 5 ml spoons) bottled
  green peppercorns, crushed
4 oz (125 g) fresh brown breadcrumbs

1 large egg (size 1–2), whisked
salt, black pepper

Prepare the leeks and slice them in thin rings. Chop the spring greens into very small pieces. Peel and finely chop the garlic. Finely chop the parsley.

Melt half the butter in a large, deep frying-pan over a medium heat. Add the leeks and stir over the heat until they have softened; then add the garlic and continue stirring for a minute. Next add the spring greens and stir for another minute or so, just until they are limp. Add the remaining butter, the tarragon and the crushed peppercorns. When the butter has melted turn the contents of the frying-pan into a bowl. Add the breadcrumbs and the chopped parsley to the mixture, followed by the whisked egg. Mix thoroughly with a wooden spoon. Season with salt and add a little black pepper.

VEAL, LEMON AND PARSLEY STUFFING

6 oz (150 g) minced veal
4 oz (100 g) fresh brown breadcrumbs
grated rind and juice of 1 large lemon
large handful of parsley – chopped finely
4 oz (100 g) melted butter
1 lightly whisked egg
salt, black pepper

Simply mix all the ingredients thoroughly together in a bowl, season well and stuff into the neck cavity of the turkey.

SAUCES

BREAD SAUCE
Serves 6–8

You can make your bread sauce several days beforehand and store it in a covered container in the fridge, stirring in the cream when you reheat it.

1 onion
4–6 cloves
1 bay leaf
1 pt (500 ml) milk
3–4 (75–100 g) fresh white breadcrumbs
2 oz (50 g) butter
2–3 gratings of a whole nutmeg
salt, black pepper
a little cream or top of the milk

Peel the onion and stick the cloves into it. Put the onion, bay leaf and milk in a pan and bring to the boil. Remove from heat, cover pan and leave for 20–30 minutes. Add the breadcrumbs and butter. Cook the sauce uncovered, over the lowest possible heat (I use an asbestos mat) for 15–20 minutes and then remove the onion and bay leaf. Season to taste with nutmeg, salt, and freshly ground black pepper. Stir in a little cream before serving.

BROWN BREAD SAUCE

Serves 6–8

I can hardly believe now that I hated bread sauce as a child (except when I see a dish of the white, glutinous mass which regrettably passes for bread sauce in too many establishments). With its combination of texture and creaminess, with soft pieces of onion and a hint of clove and nutmeg, I find that bread sauce always proves to be the most popular accompaniment to my Christmas turkey or goose. Brown bread adds both flavour and texture and in this simplest of methods you can cook the sauce either very slowly on top of the stove or in a low oven. A solid fuel cooker is ideal for this recipe if you have one. Some breads absorb more or less liquid than others, so check from time to time to see if you need add either more milk or a little more crumbled bread. You can make the sauce up to three days in advance, cover the top with greaseproof paper and keep it in the fridge to re-heat when needed. You can always remove the crusts from the bread if you don't like dark flecks in the sauce, but I think it's much nicer if you keep the crusts on.

1 large onion
5 oz (150 g) wholemeal or brown bread
3 oz (75 g) butter
6 cloves
¼ of a whole nutmeg, grated
1½ pints (900 ml) creamy milk
1½ pints (900 ml) double cream
sea salt, black pepper

Peel the onion and chop it up small. Tear the bread, including the crusts, into smallish pieces and put these with the onion into a heavy saucepan, or into an ovenproof dish if you want to cook the sauce in the oven. Dot with the butter and cloves, sprinkle with the nutmeg and season with a little salt and black pepper. Mix the milk and the cream and pout it over the other ingredients.

To cook on top of the stove, put the covered saucepan over the lowest possible heat, stirring now and then to break up the bread, for 1½–2 hours. To cook in the oven, heat the oven to Gas Mark ½/250°F/130° and put the covered dish in for 1½–2 hours, stirring round two or three times, until you have a fairly thick sauce. Lastly, check the seasoning, adjust it to taste and remove the cloves, if you can find them.

ONION, BRANDY AND ORANGE SAUCE

Serves 4–6

A lovely sauce, perfect to serve with roast goose, duck, pheasant and pork. As it is a creamy sauce, keep the pan juices from the meat separate to be served as a thin gravy.

2 large onions
3 oz (75 g) butter
1 teaspoon (5 ml spoon) ground cinnamon
coarsely grated rind of 1 and juice of 2 large oranges
1 tablespoon (15 ml spoon) plain flour
2 teaspoons (2 x 5 ml spoon) caster sugar
2–3 tablespoons (2–3 x 15 ml spoons) brandy, to taste
5 fl oz (150 ml) double cream
salt, black pepper

Peel the onions, cut them in half and then slice them as thinly as possible. Melt the butter in a large frying-pan over a low heat. Stir in the onion slices and then stir in the ground cinnamon and the orange rind. Cook gently until the onions have completely softened. Remove from the heat and stir in the flour, followed by the orange juice and the caster sugar. Return to the heat and simmer gently, stirring all the time, for about 2 minutes. Then add the brandy and the cream and continue to simmer gently, stirring, for another 3 minutes or so. Season to taste with salt and black pepper, adding more brandy if you want. Pour into a bowl to serve with your roast.

SPICED CRANBERRY AND ORANGE SAUCE

Serves 6–8

3 oz (75 g) granulated sugar
5 fl oz (125 ml) fresh orange juice
6 oz (150 g) fresh cranberries
½ teaspoon (2.5 ml spoon) cinnamon and ½ teaspoon nutmeg
or 1 teaspoon (5 ml spoon) ground allspice

Stir the sugar into the orange juice in a pan and add the cranberries and spice. Cover, bring to the boil and simmer for 5 minutes. Store in a covered container in the fridge.

APRICOT AND CLEMENTINE SAUCE FOR HAM AND OTHER COLD MEATS

Serves 4–6

A good sauce can make all the difference to cold meats. Over Christmas when one begins to tire of bland cold ham or turkey, an interesting sauce is vital to give life to the meat. The following sauce can either be served warm, which I prefer, or cold, but not chilled. Since you will probably want to make it ahead, just gently re-heat it to serve it warm.

8 oz (250 g) dried apricots
4 small clementines or small oranges
1 medium-sized onion
4–6 cloves
2 oz (50 g) soft brown sugar
water
1–2 tablespoons (1–2 x 15 ml spoon) red
*   wine vinegar*
2–4 pinches of cayenne pepper (chilli
*   powder)*

Soak the apricots in water for at least 2 hours. Then cut the unpeeled clementines or oranges across in very thin rounds, discarding any pips. Peel the onion and chop it roughly.

Put the sliced clementines, onion, cloves, sugar and the drained apricots into a saucepan and pour in water to cover. Bring the liquid to the boil, cover the pan and let it simmer very gently for about 30 minutes until soft and fairly thick. Stir vigorously to break up the apricots. Add vinegar and cayenne pepper (chilli powder) to taste.

ROAST POTATOES

Potatoes can be one of the best parts of the meal or one of the most boring. Perfect crispy roast potatoes are wonderful but particularly difficult to achieve if you only have one oven in which you are cooking the turkey at length at a low heat. However, with a little forethought, it is possible. The day before, peel your potatoes, cut them up into smaller pieces than you normally would and boil them until completely cooked.

Before you begin to roast the turkey turn the oven to Gas Mark 9/475°F/240°C. Melt lots of good dripping in a large roasting pan so that it is about 1 in.(2 cm) deep. When the fat is smoking put in the boiled potatoes and spoon the fat all over them. Put them right at the top of the oven for 20–30 minutes until they are beginning to brown and crisp. Now turn the oven down to Gas Mark 3/325°F/160°C ready for the turkey.

Put the turkey in below the potatoes. Turn the potatoes once or twice while the turkey is cooking – they should get beautifully brown and crispy all over, but roast potatoes are a bit like pastry – you are never quite sure how they'll turn out. When they look perfectly brown move them to the bottom of the oven below the turkey.

POTATOES ROASTED IN THEIR SKINS WITH OLIVE OIL

Getting your potatoes out of the roasting pan, drained of fat and into their serving dish can be a lot of trouble when you are trying to produce a turkey and all the other bits and pieces of the Christmas lunch at the same time. This way or roasting potatoes in the dish in which they are served cuts down on much of the palaver. It produces potatoes which seem more sautéd than roasted; leaving the skin on adds to both flavour and texture. If you like you can mix some very finely sliced onion amongst the potatoes before cooking them. Try to use waxy, not floury, potatoes such as the red-skinned Desirée, for this recipe as they will hold their shape far better.

The day before Christmas, cook your potatoes, whole and unpeeled, either by steaming of boiling them. While the potatoes are hot cut them up into fairly small cubes and put these in a large mixing bowl. Now, depending on how many potatoes you are cooking, pour in enough olive oil to be absorbed evenly by the hot potatoes as you turn them around with a wooden spoon. Season them with salt and black pepper. Then spoon the potatoes into a large, shallow,

THE CHRISTMAS DINNER

ovenproof dish and leave in a cool place until needed.

If possible cook the potatoes in a hot oven at Gas Mark 9/475°F/240°C on the top shelf for 20–30 minutes at the beginning, turning them around gently before continuing to cook them at a lower temperature. In any case let them cook above the turkey until you think they look brown and crisp enough, and then put them under the turkey at the bottom of the oven where they should gently crisp up some more but not become too browned.

VEGETABLES

All I can say about your vegetables is : don't overcook them. I think it is much more important to cook one vegetable perfectly, rather than several badly because you are too busy. I buy the smallest sprouts I can find, prepare them the day before – but cook at the last moment for 5–6 minutes only so that they are still slightly crisp and bright green. It is now possible to buy circular steamers which expand or contract to fit any size saucepan. Vegetables cooked in this simple way taste much better and the goodness doesn't seep away into the water.

BROAD BEANS AND ALMONDS IN CHIVE CREAM
Serves 6

If you are tired of having Brussels sprouts with your turkey every Christmas or want an extra vegetable which doesn't take long to prepare, try this mixture.

> 1 lb (400 g) frozen broad beans
> 3–4 oz (75–100 g) whole blanched
>   almonds
> a good knob of butter
> 1 carton fresh soured cream
> 2 rounded teaspoons (2 x 5 ml spoon)
>   dried chives

Boil the broad beans in salted water until cooked. Drain, put into a serving dish with the almonds and dot with butter. Stir the chives into the soured cream and spoon it over the broad beans. Cover the dish and keep warm until you eat, giving it a stir just before you start so that the cream coats the beans and nuts well.

COOKING FOR CHRISTMAS

TRADITIONAL CHRISTMAS PUDDING

Makes 2 puddings, each feeding 8–10 people

This is an old North Country recipe for a dark, moist full- flavoured pudding. I make it every year and it seems to have just the right mature, traditional flavour.

4 oz (100 g) self-raising flour
½ teaspoon (2.5 ml spoon) salt
1 teaspoon (5 ml spoon) mixed spice
1 teaspoon (5 ml spoon) ground cinnamon
½-¾ of a whole nutmeg – grated
½ teaspoon (2.5 ml spoon) ground cloves
8 oz (200 g) shredded suet
10 oz (250 g) fresh white breadcrumbs
grated rind and juice of 1 lemon and 1 orange
½ lb (200 g) demerara sugar
½ lb (200 g) grated carrots
½ lb (200 g) grated cooking apples
12 oz (300 g) raisins
8 oz (200 g) currants
8 oz (200 g) sultanas
4 oz (100 g) mixed peel
2 oz (50 g) flaked almonds
2 tablespoons (2 × 15 ml spoon) black treacle
½ large wineglass Cointreau or brandy
4 lightly whisked eggs (size 4)

Sieve the flour, salt and spice into a large mixing bowl. Add all the remaining dry ingredients. Mix together thoroughly. Melt the treacle in a pan to make it a little runny. Stir into it the lemon and orange juice and the Cointreau or brandy and finally the eggs. Pour the liquid into the pudding mixture and stir thoroughly. Cover the bowl with a cloth and leave until the next day. Butter two 2-pt pudding basins and spoon in the mixture. Cover with a double layer of buttered greaseproof paper and then either a cloth tied on with string or foil tucked in round the rim.

Steam for 5–6 hours in pans of simmering water which should be kept topped up two-thirds up the sides of the basins. When cool, re-cover the basins and store in a cool place. On Christmas Day steam for a further 2–3 hours.

THE BEST CHRISTMAS PUDDING
Makes 1 large and 1 small pudding

This is certainly the best pudding I have eaten. Because it has no sugar and no flour it is lighter in texture than usual and much more palatable after a rich meal.

butter, for greasing
3 oz (75 g) glace cherries
6 oz (175 g) candied peel
12 oz (375 g) seedless raisins
6 oz (175 g) pitted prunes, roughly
  chopped
6 oz (175 g) currants
3 oz (75 g) walnut pieces
8 oz (250 g) fresh white breadcrumbs
8 oz (250 g) shredded suet
1 teaspoon (5ml spoon) ground
  cinnamon
¼ whole nutmeg, grated
6 eggs
2 oranges, juice and coarsely grated rind
¼ pint (150 ml) stout
3 tablespoons (3 x 15 ml spoons) brandy,
  rum or whisky

Generously butter a 2-pint (1.1-litre) and a 1-pint (600 ml) pudding basin. Chop up the glacé cherries roughly. Put the dried fruit, walnuts, orange rind, breadcrumbs, suet and spices in a large bowl and mix thoroughly.

Whisk the eggs until frothy and thicken and stir into the dried ingredients. Lastly stir in the orange juice, stout and spirits, adding enough to make a mixture which just drops from the spoon.

Spoon the mixture into the pudding basins and smooth the tops. Cover each basin with a double layer of well buttered foil and tie tightly with string, making a string handle to lift out the basin. Put the basins, preferably on racks or inverted saucers, into large saucepans and pout in boiling water to come three-quarters of the way up the sides of each basin. Cover the pan and steam, for about 6 hours for the larger basin and 4-5 hours for the smaller, checking to see if the water needs topping up after about 2 hours.

When the puddings are cold, put them away in a dark, cool place, where they will keep for 2-3 months if necessary. On Christmas Day, replace the buttered foil with clean layers and steam for another hour or so before serving with brandy butter or whipped cream.

CHOCOLATE CRUNCH CHRISTMAS PUDDING

Serves 8–10

If you are not insistent on sticking to tradition you can make this, which is not a Christmas pudding at all (it is crunchy and cold instead of soft and hot) but it looks perfect as an alternative on Christmas Day. It also has the advantage of being extremely quick to make and is much more popular than Christmas pudding with most children, and several adults too. It is expensive on chocolate but rich and filling and goes a long way.

For the pudding

6 oz (150 g) butter or margarine
3 tablespoons (3 × 15 ml spoon) golden
   syrup
8 oz (200 g) plain chocolate
6 oz (150 g) crushed ginger biscuits
6 oz (150 g) crushed plain sweet biscuits
1 oz (25 g) currants
3 oz (75 g) raisins
2 oz (50 g) glacé cherries – roughly
   chopped
1 oz (25 g) candied peel
2 teaspoons (2 × 5 ml spoon) ground
   cinnamon
2 tablespoons (2 × 15 ml spoon) brandy
   or rum

For the icing and decoration

3 oz (75 g) plain chocolate
1 tablespoon (15 ml spoon) water
1 oz (25 g) butter or margarine
a little icing sugar, 2–3 halved glacé
   cherries and a sprig of holly for
   decoration

Grease a 2-pt pudding basin. Gently melt and stir together the butter, syrup and chocolate in a saucepan. Mix in the rest of the ingredients and spoon into the pudding basin. Chill in the refrigerator until set. Then dip the basin briefly in hot water and turn the pudding out.

To make the icing, gently melt the chocolate with the water and stir until smooth, add the butter and stir until melted in. Cool very slightly and then ice the pudding all over with the chocolate. When cold, sprinkle a little icing sugar over the top of the pudding (to look like a sprinkling of snow!), stick in the sprig of holly and press the glacé cherries in a cluster round it. Keep in a cool place, but not in the fridge. Serve, with cream, cut into slices with a sharp knife.

THE CHRISTMAS DINNER

RUM BUTTER

Serves 6–8

When I was a child and didn't like Christmas pudding very much the only reason I would eat a spoonful was to have a huge dollop of rum or brandy butter on the top. Now my children feel the same. If you prefer brandy butter make it with icing sugar and brandy. You can make the butter when you make the pudding, pack it into a plastic box with a lid and store it in your refrigerator. Take out well beforehand on Christmas Day.

> 8 oz (200 g) unsalted butter
> 4–6 oz (100–150 g) (to taste) soft, pale brown sugar
> 4–5 tablespoons (4–5 × 15 ml spoon) light rum

Cream the butter until pale and soft. Beat in the sugar. Add the rum drop by drop, beating all the time so that it doesn't curdle.

CHILLED BRANDY SAUCE

Serves 6–8

This quickly made, light and creamy sauce is an alternative to rum or brandy butter with the Christmas pudding – in fact, it's delicious with almost any hot pudding.

> ¼ pt (125 ml) double cream
> 1 level tablespoon (15 ml spoon) icing sugar – sifted
> 1–2 tablespoons (1–2 x 15 ml spoon) brandy

Simply whisk the cream until thick, then whisk in the icing sugar and gradually stir in the brandy to taste. Chill in the refrigerator.

FIRST COURSES AND SNACKS

I have given up having a first course to the Christmas dinner since it's always such a noisy and chaotic meal, with the over-excitment of the children and the table covered with decorations and crackers, not to mention many dishes of food. A first course just over-complicates things and everyone has far too much to eat anyway. However, eating leads to more eating and my family's appetites seem to double during those few festive days. The following dishes are useful at other meals, for friends dropping in or for a lighter lunch or supper.

CHICKEN LIVER AND ALMOND PÂTÉ
Serves 6–8

Chicken liver pâté is one of the easiest to make, but I have always found the taste slightly strong and the texture a little smooth. However, this is a mild version in which the orange juice and cream soften the strong liver taste and the chopped almonds give a crunchiness to the texture. If you are not using it in a stuffing you can use the liver from your turkey in this recipe.

4 oz (100 g) unsalted butter
1 small onion – chopped finely
8 oz (200 g) chicken livers
1 rounded teaspoon mild French mustard
1 level teaspoon (5 ml spoon) ground nutmeg

salt, black pepper
2 tablespoons (2 × 15 ml spoon) brandy
juice of ½ orange
2 tablespoons (2 × 15 ml spoon) cream
1 oz (25 g) chopped blanched almonds
1 teaspoon (5 ml spoon) fresh or dried chives (optional)

Melt 1 oz (25 g) butter in a frying pan and gently cook the onion until soft. Add the chicken livers and cook gently, stirring once or twice for 5 minutes. Add the mustard and nutmeg, a further 2 oz (50 g) butter, salt and pepper. When the butter has melted, remove from the heat and add the brandy, orange juice and cream. Whizz up in a liquidiser until smooth, or press through a sieve. Stir the chopped almonds into the mixture and all but a sprinkling of the chives. Transfer to an earthenware dish and sprinkle top with the remaining chives.

Gently bubble the remaining 1 oz (25 g) butter in a pan for a minute. Remove from the heat and let stand for another minute or two. Then pour the melted butter through a fine sieve or coffee strainer over the top of the pâté. Let cool. Then cover with foil and chill well in the fridge before serving with thin toast.

LAYERED SARDINE LOAF
Serves 8–10

This unusual fish pâté has every advantage. Firstly, it is delicious. It is easy to make and inexpensive. It freezes well or can be made and chilled in the fridge a day in advance. Lastly, with its dark green parsley and butter top, it has an extremely impressive appearance. It is perfect either as a first course or as an accompaniment to cold meats.

4 oz (100 g) butter or block margarine
1 lb (400 g) cream cheese – at room
temperature

2 tins sardines
juice of ½ lemon
2–3 cloves garlic – crushed or chopped
finely
salt, black pepper
good handful of parsley – chopped finely
approx. 1 small loaf wholemeal or granary
bread – sliced thinly

Butter a loaf tin, size about 9 in. × 5 in. (23 cm × 13 cm). Melt 3 oz (75 g) butter and leave it to cool a bit. Put in the cream cheese in a mixing bowl and mash the sardines into it with a wooden spoon. Stir in the lemon juice, garlic and melted butter bit by bit. Add salt and plenty of black pepper. Mix all together thoroughly. Melt the remaining 1 oz (25 g) butter and stir into it the chopped parsley. Spread this mixture on the bottom of the loaf tin. Cut the rinds off the slices of bread and cut to shape to make a layer of bread on top of the parsley, then spread a rather thick layer of the cream cheese mixture over the bread, then another layer of bread, and so on, ending with a layer of bread. Cover with foil or plastic film and chill overnight in the fridge.

To turn out, dip the tin briefly in hot water and slip the loaf on to a serving dish. If necessary smooth the sides with a knife. Chill again in the fridge until needed.

FEATHERLIGHT CHEESE BISCUITS

The adults can nibble these with their Christmas drinks and the children, who love making them, can just nibble them! They will keep crisp in an airtight tin.

6 oz (150 g) grated cheese
4 oz (100 g) plain wholemeal flour.
2 level teaspoons (2 × 5 ml spoon)
   baking powder
2 teaspoons (2 × 5 ml spoon) paprika (or
   variations – either 1 rounded teaspoon
   (2 × 5 ml spoon) curry powder or 1 level
   teaspoon (5 ml spoon) caraway seeds)
4 oz (100 g) butter or margarine
2 egg yolks

Preheat oven to Gas Mark 7/425°F/220°C. Put the grated cheese into a mixing bowl. Sift the flour with the baking powder and paprika into the cheese. Cut the butter into small pieces and rub into the flour and cheese with your fingertips. Add the egg yolks and mix with a wooden spoon to a stiff dough. Gather into a ball, press out with your hands on a floured board and roll out to about ½ in. (1 cm) thick. Cut into small biscuits with a 2 in. (5 cm) cutter or the rim of a glass. Place on a large ungreased baking sheet. Bake at the top of the oven for 8–12 minutes until light golden brown. Cool before removing from the baking sheet.

STUFFED CHEESE SHORTBREAD

As a snack or to liven up a leftovers meal of bits and pieces these light, crunchy biscuits, combined with a creamy cheese and chive mixture, are very tempting. You can make the biscuits days before and keep them in an airtight tin until you need them, and of course you can eat them just on their own.

For the biscuits

6 oz (150 g) plain flour
1 teaspoon (5 ml spoon) salt
3 oz (75 g) fine semolina
For the spread
4 oz (100 g) strong cheddar cheese –
   grated finely
6 oz (150 g) butter – at room temperature
6 oz (150 g) cream cheese
1 tablespoon (15 ml spoon) chopped
   dried chives or spring onions
black pepper

Heat oven to Gas Mark 2/300°F/150°C. Lightly grease a large baking sheet or tin. Mix the flour, salt and semolina together in a bowl. Add the cheese and butter. Work the mixture together thoroughly with your fingers until you have a smooth dough. Roll out thickly – about ½ in. (1 cm) - on a floured board and cut into small biscuits with a 2 in. (5 cm) cutter or the rim of a glass. Arrange on the baking sheet and bake in the centre of the oven for 1 hour. Allow to cool a little and then transfer the biscuits to a wire tray to cool completely.

To make the cream cheese mixture, simply soften the cream cheese with a fork and mix in the chopped chives and black pepper to taste. Use either to sandwich together the biscuits or just to spread on top of them.

CREAMY AUBERGINE PURÉE
Serves 6

This most delicious cold purée from Turkey is deceptively easy to make and aubergines are plentiful in the shops during the winter. It is very light in texture and has a distinctive smoky taste. Serve it as a first course with toast, as a dip at a buffet or simply as a snack.

2 medium-size aubergines
juice of ½ lemon
approx 3 tablespoons (3 × 15 ml spoon)
    sunflower oil
salt, black pepper
a little chopped parsley to garnish

Put the aubergines, unpeeled, under a very

hot grill, turning them once or twice until the skin is black and beginning to blister. This will probably take 15–25 minutes. Now peel off all the skin. As they will be hot this is easier to do under cold water. Put them in a large sieve and press them down with a wooden spoon or a plate so that as much juice as possible comes out of them. They will now look like old rags, but don't worry, a miraculous transformation is about to take place! Put them into the liquidiser with the lemon juice. Whizz up and add the sunflower oil a little at a time until the mixture is smooth, pale and very light. The more oil you add, the lighter the texture.

Add salt and pepper to taste. Store in a covered plastic dish in the fridge for up to a week, or freeze. To serve, spoon into a bowl and sprinkle on a little chopped parsley.

KIPPER AND ONION QUICHE WITH CHEESE PASTRY

Serves 6–8

A good quiche is always popular and this one, made with kipper fillets, is a tasty contrast to all the meat and turkey one eats at Christmas time. You can make the quiche in advance – it freezes well. Warmed up and accompanied simply by a crisp green salad it makes an effortless supper dish on Christmas Eve.

For a change, replace kippers with smoked mackerel fillets.

For the pastry

10 oz (250 g) plain flour
good pinch of salt
5 oz (125 g) butter or margarine
2 oz (50 g) lard
3 oz (75 g) grated cheese
1 lightly whisked egg (size 3)

For the filling

3 eggs and 1 extra yolk (size 3)
approx. ¼ pt (125 ml) single cream or
   milk
salt, black pepper
2 large onions
1 oz (25 g) butter or margarine for frying
2–3 (according to size) kipper fillets

Sift the flour and salt into a mixing bowl. Cut the butter and lard into the flour and rub with your fingertips until it is like breadcrumbs. Stir in the grated cheese with a knife, then the egg and a very little cold water until the mixture just sticks together. Gather into a ball, wrap in foil and cool in the fridge for at least half an hour. Then roll the pastry on a floured board and line a buttered 9 in. (23 cm) flan dish with it. Prick the base of the pastry lightly with a fork.

To make the filling, whisk the eggs lightly and mix in a bowl with the cream, salt and black pepper. Chop the onions into small pieces and fry gently in butter or margarine until soft and transparent. Scrape the kipper flesh from the skin, remove any bones and flake it into the cream-and-egg mixture. Stir in the fried onion. Pour the mixture into the pastry case and bake in the centre of a preheated oven at Gas Mark 5/375°F/190°C for 30–40 minutes until just firm in the centre.

BLACK PEARL MUSHROOMS
Serves 6

The rich feasts at Christmas hardly need first courses but something really light and titillating like this, which takes no time to prepare, is a useful idea to have up your sleeve. Serve with crusty brown bread to mop up the juices

1lb (500 g) mushrooms
a bunch of spring onions
3 garlic cloves
6 tablespoons (6 x 15 ml spoon) olive oil
   or sunflower oil
coarsely grated rind and juice of 1 lemon
1 tablespoon (15 ml spoon) red wine
   vinegar
a handful of finely chopped parsley
a pot of Danish lumpfish caviare
a bunch of watercress
salt, black pepper

Slice the mushrooms fairly thinly. Cut the roots off the spring onions and chop the rest into 1-inch (2.5 cm) pieces using as much of the green part as possible. Peel the garlic cloves and slice them across very thinly.

Put the oil into a large, deep frying-pan over a medium heat, add the sliced garlic and stir it around for a minute or so; add the sliced spring onions and the grated lemon rind and stir for a minute more. Next add the lemon juice, the wine vinegar and the sliced mushrooms to the pan. Stir for a minute or two until the mushrooms are just beginning to soften. Remove the pan from the heat, add plenty of black pepper and stir in the chopped parsley. Turn the mixture into a bowl and when it has cooled, stir in the Danish lumpfish caviar; check for seasoning and add a little salt only if necessary. Keep in the bowl, covered in the fridge.

When ready to eat, spoon the mixture on to a serving plate and pick the leaves off the watercress stems to use in bunches as a border round the mushroom mixture.

SMOKED FISH AND ALMOND MOUSSE
Serves 6–8

This light mousse is topped with crisp almond flakes. It makes a good contrast to the Christmas meat and turkey, either as a first course or eaten with the cold meats. It is easy to make if you have a liquidiser, and you can either freeze it or make it a day or two beforehand. It should be served well chilled.

> 1 lb (400 g) smoked cod or whiting fillets
> 2 lightly whisked eggs
> 3 tablespoons (3 × 15 ml spoon) milk
> juice of ½ lemon
> 1 oz (25 g) butter
> 2 oz (50 g) flaked almonds
> ½ pt (250 ml) double cream
> 2 teaspoons (2 × 5 ml spoon) dried fennel, oregano or tarragon
> salt, black pepper

Heat oven to Gas Mark 4/350°/180°C. Put a roasting pan full of hot water on the centre shelf. Chop the fish roughly and remove any skin. Drop the eggs and milk into the liquidiser. Add about a quarter of the fish and whizz up until smooth and then add the lemon juice and the rest of the fish bit by bit, whizzing after each addition. As it gets very thick you will probably have to stop and stir it around now and then to make sure it all turns to a smooth purée. Transfer to a bowl. Melt the butter in a pan and quickly stir the flaked almonds around it until well coated. Remove from heat. Whisk up the cream until fairly thick, not stiff, and stir gently into the fish purée. Season with herbs, a little salt and plenty of black pepper.

Butter a soufflé dish and spoon the mixture into it. Smooth top and sprinkle with the butter-coated almonds. Put the dish in the pan of water in the oven and cook for 25–30 minutes. Leave to cool and chill well before serving.

VEGETABLE CONSOMMÉ WITH SHREDDED LETTUCE
Serves 4–6

The lightest possible kind of soup can be useful to have in the house at Christmas. It could be the answer, either at the end of the day of overeating when you simply don't want another big meal, or an appetizing but not too filling course.

> 1 large onion
> 1lb (500 g) tomatoes
> 12 oz (375 g) carrots
> 2½ pints (1.5 litres) water

2 teaspoons (2 x 5 ml spoon) caster
  sugar
2 Little Gem lettuces or 2 lettuce hearts
3-4 tablespoons dry sherry
salt, black pepper

Wash the onion but don't peel it. Then cut it into eight. Cut up the tomatoes and carrots roughly. Put all the vegetables into a saucepan and pour in the water. Season with salt and black pepper and the caster sugar. Cover the pan, bring it to the boil and simmer for about 1½ hours.

Line a large sieve with a thin, clean linen tea cloth and put it over another saucepan. Pour the soup into the sieve, pushing gently with a wide wooden spoon to get all the liquid through the sieve and the tea cloth. Check the soup for seasoning and discard the vegetables. Before re-heating the soup, slice the lettuces across as thinly as you can. Bring the soup to boiling point, add the shredded lettuce, bubble for half a minute only, and then remove from the heat. Stir in the sherry to taste and serve. White bowls look prettiest for the clear, golden soup.

WALNUT SOUP
Serves 6

What with everything else both to eat and prepare over Christmas, elaborate first courses seem to be to be quite unnecessary. On the other hand, a good soup is a perfect start to a lunch or supper of cold turkey, meats or pâtés. Soups can, of course, be made ahead and re-heated very quickly, which makes them all the more practical for the Christmas period. This is an excellent, creamy winter soup of walnuts and soft, sweet onion that goes well with all Christmassy foods.

1 large onion
2 tablespoons (2 x 15 ml spoon) olive oil
1 oz (25 g) butter
4 oz (125 g) walnut pieces
1 level tablespoon (15 ml spoon) caster
  sugar
1 level tablespoon (15 ml spoon) ground
  mace
1 oz (25 g) plain flour
1 pint (600 ml) good chicken or turkey
  stock
1¼ pints (750 ml) milk
a handful of finely chopped parsley
5 fl oz (142ml) carton of soured cream
salt, black pepper

Peel the onion, cut it in half and slice it as thinly as possible. Put the olive oil with the butter in a large, heavy saucepan and melt the butter over a medium heat. Add the sliced onion and cook, stirring frequently, for 10 minutes or so until it is softened and slightly browned. Meanwhile, put the walnut pieces in a food processor and grind them finely; don't leave the machine on too long or the nuts will stick together and become oily.

When the onion has softened, remove the pan from the heat and stir in the caster sugar, the ground mace and the ground walnuts. Then stir in the flour. Gradually add the chicken or turkey stock and the milk. Put the saucepan back on the heat and bring it to the boil, stirring frequently. Let it bubble, stirring all the time for 2–3 minutes; then cover the pan and let it simmer very gently for 20 minutes. Adjust the seasoning to taste with black pepper and salt. Before serving, stir the chopped parsley into the soup, and, when it has been ladled out into soup plates, spoon some soured cream on to the soup in each plate.

CELERY AND WALNUT PIES
Makes 18 little pies

These light little pies should be served hot but they can be made ahead and re-heated. Serve them, if you like, as a first course; I make a cold sauce to accompany them from a can of chopped tomatoes, seasoned with a real bite of cayenne pepper (chilli powder) and a little lemon juice; or serve them as something to nibble during one of the drinking moments of Christmas. The pies have a flaky, cheesy pastry which is quickly made.

For the filling
2 celery hearts, weighing about 12–14 oz
   (375–425 g) in total
3 large garlic cloves
2 oz (50 g) butter
1 teaspoon (5 ml spoon) dill seeds
1 tablespoon (15 ml spoon) plain flour
8 fl oz (250 ml) milk
2 rounded teaspoons (2 x 5 ml rounded
   spoons) whole-seed mustard
18 walnut halves
3–4 good pinches of cayenne pepper
   (chilli powder)
salt

For the pastry

8 oz (250 g) plain flour, plus extra for
rolling
½ –1 teaspoon (2.5–5 ml spoon) salt
about 6 oz (175 g) frozen butter
2 oz (50 g) mature Cheddar cheese,
grated coarsely
6–7 tablespoons (6–7 x 15 ml spoons)
cold water
milk

Make the filling first. Chop the celery hearts into small pieces. Peel and chop the garlic finely. Melt the butter in a largish frying-pan, add the celery and cook it over a gentle heat, stirring now and then, for 10–15 minutes, until soft. Then add the chopped garlic and the dill seeds and continue cooking for another 5 minutes. Remove the pan from the heat and stir in the flour. Then gradually stir in the milk. Put the pan back on the heat and let it bubble, stirring all the time, for about 3 minutes, until thickened. Stir in the mustard. Season to taste with salt and the cayenne pepper (chilli powder). Turn into a bowl, cover with a piece of greaseproof paper and leave on one side to cool.

Now make the pastry. Sift the flower and salt into a bowl. Holding the block of frozen butter in a cloth at one end, grate if coarsely, mixing it into the flour a bit at a time with a fork.

Then fork in the grated cheese. Finally mix in the cold water with a fork until the dough begins to stick together. Gently press it together into a ball and leave it in the fridge for 30 minutes or more.

Roll out just under three-quarters of the dough on a floured surface to about 1/8 -inch (3 mm) thick. Cut out 18 rounds with a 3-inch (7.5 cm) diameter pastry cutter and line the tins. Pile a heaped tablespoon of the filling in each round and then place a half-walnut on top of the filling. Roll out the remaining dough and, using a 2½-inch (6.5 cm) cutter, cut out another 18 rounds to top the pies. Put the tops on and press the edges to seal. Cut a slit in the top of each pie for the steam to escape.

Heat the oven to Gas Mark 7/425°F/220°C. Brush the tops of the pies with milk. Cook them in the centre of the oven for 15–20 minutes until golden brown. After removing them from the oven leave the pies to rest in the tins for 8–10 minutes before gently easing them out with a knife and transferring them to a cooling rack, or a plate if you are serving them immediately.

SMOKED OYSTER SURPRISES

Serves 6–10

You can serve these stuffed pork meatballs at a pre-Christmas supper for six, accompanied by vegetables or simply by bread and salad, but I like them best as a snack if friends come over for a drink, in which case they would serve about ten people. If you want to make them ahead, they also taste good eaten cold.

> 1¼ lb (625 g) lean minced pork
> 1 large garlic clove
> 1-inch (2.5 cm) piece of fresh ginger
> 2 rounded teaspoons (2 x 5 ml rounded spoons) whole-seed mustard
> 3½ oz (105 g) can of smoked oysters
> 1 tablespoon (15 ml spoon) sunflower oil
> salt, black pepper

Put the minced pork into a bowl. Peel the garlic and ginger, chop them together finely and then mix them into the pork, with the mustard, a sprinkling of salt and a generous grinding of black pepper. Drain the oysters, reserving the oil. Take up small handfuls of the pork mixture and flatten them out into circles like little hamburgers. Place a smoked oyster in the centre and wrap the meat up round the oyster to enclose it. Form into a ball.

Continue like this until the meat is used up and then smear the oil from the oyster can over the meatballs. Heat the sunflower oil in a large frying-pan over a medium heat. Fry the meatballs for about 15 minutes, turning them gently, until they are browned all over.

SPROUT SNOW

Serves 6

This is really just a way of using up leftover brussels sprouts; in this recipe they are made into a light mousse which can be served as a first course or as part of a meal. You should only use sprouts which have not been over-cooked and which are still bright green.

> 3 tablespoons (3 x 15 ml spoon) water
> 1/3 oz (11 g) sachet of gelatine
> ½ pint (300 ml) milk
> 3 large eggs (size 1–2)
> ¼ of a whole nutmeg, grated
> 12 oz (375 g) lightly cooked sprouts
> chopped parsley
> salt, black pepper

Put the water in a small bowl and sprinkle in the gelatine. Set the bowl in a pan of water over a low heat and stir until the gelatine dissolves. Allow to cool. Put the milk into a saucepan and bring to the boil. Remove from the heat. Separate the eggs, putting the whites in a large bowl and the yolks in the top of a double saucepan (or into a mixing bowl which you can set over a pan of water). Pour the hot milk on to the egg yolks, whisking thoroughly. Put the egg yolks and milk over a saucepan of gently simmering water and stir constantly with a wooden spoon until thickened to a custard. Turn the custard into a large bowl and season it heavily with black pepper and salt. Stir in the grated nutmeg and allow to cool. Stir in the gelatine.

Now chop up the sprouts finely and stir them into the custard. Whisk the egg whites to soft peaks and then fold them into the sprout mixture and turn into a 1½–2-pint (900 ml– 1.2-litre) ring mould or loaf tin. Refrigerate until set. Twenty minutes before serving, dip the mould or tin briefly in a sink of hot water and then turn it out, giving it a good shake, on to a serving plate. Sprinkle the top with chopped parsley.

HOT MAIN DISHES

If your family arrive on Christmas Eve it's nice to have a dish which prepares their taste buds for the treats in store and which will put them in a festive mood. Through the holiday you may need one or two good hot dishes which contrast well with the other Christmas tastes, and after one or two meals of eating up the cold turkey and meats a sizzling hot dish becomes very welcome again.

ROAST PORK WITH TOMATO AND TARRAGON SAUCE

Serves 6–8

If you like to have a joint of pork at Christmas, it can be enormously enhanced by an interesting sauce instead of the usual brown gravy. This rich tomato sauce is no trouble to make but adds greatly to the succulence and flavour of the meat.

1 3–4 lb (1.2–1.6 kg) joint pork on the bone
3–4 cloves garlic – chopped finely
juice of 1 lemon
sunflower or groundnut oil
salt, black pepper

For the sauce
1 tin tomatoes
1 large glass red wine

2 teaspoons (2 × 5 ml spoon) French mustard
1 teaspoon (5 ml spoon) sugar
2 teaspoons (2 × 5 ml spoon) dried tarragon
juices from the meat
1 dessertspoon (10 ml spoon) cornflour
salt, black pepper

Make deep incisions in the meat and poke the chopped garlic in as far as you can. If not already done by the butcher, score the thick fat closely with a sharp knife. Mix the lemon juice and twice as much oil with salt and black pepper in a cup and smear all over the meat. Put the joint in a roasting pan and if possible cover the meat with foil.

Leave for at least two hours at room temperature, spooning the juices over the meat again once or twice.

Heat the oven to Gas Mark 9/475°F/240°C. Remove foil from the meat. Rub the scored fat with salt and a little extra oil (this should produce golden crisp crackling) and roast at the high heat for 20 minutes, then turn down the oven to Gas Mark 3/325°F/160°C and cook for a further 2–2¼ hours.

Before the meat is quite ready, put the tomatoes, wine, mustard, sugar and tarragon into a saucepan. Blend the cornflour until smooth with a little water and add to the mixture. Bring to the boil, stirring, and bubble for 2–3 minutes. Add salt and black pepper to taste.

When the meat is ready, pour the excess fat from the pan and add the meat juices to the sauce. If the sauce seems too thick add a little more wine or water. Pour the sauce into a serving jug and pour over the meat when carved.

RED VELVET CASSEROLE OF BEEF
Serves 6–8

A precooked casserole is useful to have ready over Christmas to heat up when everyone is tired of cold turkey. This flavourful beef, wrapped thickly in a smooth red sauce, looks particularly festive.

> *rind and juice of 1 large orange*
> *1 lb (400 g) cooked beetroot*
> *1 level tablespoon (15 ml spoon) sugar*
> *2–3 cloves garlic*
> *½ pt (250 ml) water*
> *1¾-2 lb (700–800 g) best stewing steak*
> *1 oz (25 g) butter*
> *2 tablespoons (2 × 15 ml spoon) olive or*
>   *sunflower oil*
> *2 rounded teaspoons (4 × 5 ml spoon)*
>   *ground ginger*
> *1 rounded tablespoon (2 × 15 ml spoon)*
>   *plain flour*
> *salt, black pepper*
> *1 carton fresh soured cream*

Grate the orange rind. Roughly chop the beetroot and put into a liquidiser with the orange juice, orange rind, sugar, garlic and water. Whizz to a smooth purée. You may need to do this quantity in two goes. Cut up the stewing steak into largish slices.

Melt the butter and oil together in an iron-based casserole on top of the stove or in a large saucepan. Stir the meat into the melted fat and sprinkle on the ground ginger. Remove from heat and stir in a level tablespoonful of plain flour. Heat the beetroot purée and stir into the beef. If you are already using a casserole put on the lid and cook in a preheated oven at Gas Mark 1/275°F/140°C for 2–2½ hours or until the beef is tender (if you started in a saucepan transfer the mixture to a casserole). Check for seasoning and add salt and pepper.

Just before serving, spoon the soured cream over the top. Serve with baked potatoes or rice and a green vegetable or salad.

DUCK WITH GOOSEBERRY AND BRAZIL NUT STUFFING
Serves 4–6

If you are a small family and decide to have duck at Christmas, this gooseberry and nut stuffing and sauce makes a nice change from the traditional orange sauce. Made in a slightly larger quantity it is also good for goose.

1 4½-5½ lb (1.75–2.25 kg) duck

For the stuffing
2 oz (50 g) pearl barley
coarsely grated rind and juice of 1 small orange
drained gooseberries from 1 small tin
heart and liver of the duck – chopped finely
2 oz (50 g) brazil nuts – chopped finely
2 oz (50 g) melted butter
1 lightly whisked egg (size 4)
salt, black pepper

For the sauce
juice from the tin of gooseberries
1 small glass sweet vermouth or sherry
juices from the duck
approx. 2 level teaspoons (2 × 5 ml spoon) arrowroot or cornflour
salt, black pepper

Boil the pearl barley in unsalted water, until tender but still slightly nutty. Rinse through with cold water and then mix thoroughly with the rest of the stuffing ingredients. Season well. Stuff the whole of the duck with this mixture and truss up or stick skewers in to keep down the loose skin of the neck and hold the legs together. Heat oven to Gas Mark 6/400°F/200°C. Rub a little salt all over the skin of the duck and roast in the centre of the oven, first on one side for 30 minutes then the other side for 30 minutes and finally on its back for 40–50 minutes.

Transfer the duck to a serving plate and keep warm. Then pour off the fat from the juices (keep the fat, as it is wonderful for fried and roast potatoes) and pour the juices into a saucepan. Add the gooseberry juice and vermouth. Blend the arrowroot (this will make a transparent, shiny sauce) or cornflour with a little water and stir into the juices. Bring to the boil and bubble, stirring, for 2–3 minutes. Season with salt and pepper. Serve in a sauce jug with the duck. Don't forget to spoon all the delicious stuffing out.

SPICY BEEF AND GUINNESS PIE
Serves 6–8

A golden pie which looks and tastes extra-special. It is most suitable for one of your festive meals as it can be prepared well beforehand and will only need putting into the oven to bake. If you have an aversion to prunes don't be put off – they disintegrate in the stout and produce the most delicious, rich, dark sauce. The juniper berries are optional but can be found in most delicatessens and will add tantalisingly to the flavour. Allspice is best ground from whole berries but you can also buy it ground (just to muddle you it is sometimes known as Pimento or Jamaica pepper). If you can't find allspice use more nutmeg and two more cloves. For the top you can use packet puff pastry if you like but the easy flaky pastry is very little trouble and beautifully crisp. Make your pastry first or while the pie filling is cooking.

For the easy flaky pastry
8 oz (200 g) plain flour
good pinch salt
*6 oz (150 g) from an 8 oz block frozen
    butter or margarine*
*6 tablespoons (6 × 15 ml spoon) very
    cold water – preferably
chilled in the fridge*
For the glaze – 1 egg yolk

For the pie filling

1 teaspoon (5 ml spoon) whole allspice
  berries
6 cloves
1 teaspoon (5 ml spoon) juniper berries
  (optional)
1 tablespoon (15 ml spoon) oil
¼ - ½ whole nutmeg – grated
2–3 large cloves garlic – chopped finely
2 lb (800 g) lean stewing beef – chopped
  in cubes
½ pt bottle Guinness or other stout
8 oz (200 g) large prunes – soaked in
  water overnight
1 lb (400 g) carrots – cleaned and sliced
salt, black pepper
2 teaspoons (2 × 5 ml spoon) arrowroot

To make the pastry, sift the flour and salt into a bowl. Put a grater into the bowl on top of the flour. Hold the frozen butter in its wrapping and coarsely grate off 6 oz (three-quarters of the block). With a palette knife mix the fat into the flour until crumbly. Now add the water gradually, mixing again with the knife and then gather the dough up with your hands into a ball. Wrap in foil or polythene and put in the fridge for at least an hour.

Heat the oven to Gas Mark 1/275°F/140°C. Crush the allspice and cloves together in a pestle and mortar or in a coffee grinder, add the juniper berries and crush roughly. Heat the oil in the bottom of an iron casserole. Put the crushed spices together with the grated nutmeg and chopped garlic into the hot oil and stir over the heat for ½ minute. Add the beef and just seal all over for 2–3 minutes over a high heat. Stir in the stout and ½ cup water.

Remove the stones from the soaked prunes and add. Bring to the boil and then cover the dish and cook in the oven at Gas Mark 1/275°F/140°C for an hour. (Make the pastry now if you haven't already.) Then add the carrots and continue cooking for a further 1–1½ hours until the meat is tender. Season to taste with salt and black pepper.

Blend the arrowroot with a spot of water and stir in. Bubble for a minute or two on top of the stove. Then pour into a 2½-pt pie dish and leave until cold. When the filling is cold, roll out the pastry on a floured surface to roughly the size and shape of the pie dish.

Moisten the edge of the dish and lay the pastry on top. Cut round the edges and press down lightly. Roll out the trimmings and use to make a pattern, or cut-out letters to read "*Happy Christmas*"! Cover the pastry loosely with plastic film or foil and put the complete dish in the fridge until the next day, or in the freezer (if the freezer, remember to defrost before baking).

To bake, heat the oven to Gas Mark 7/425°F/220°C. Brush the pastry all over with egg yolk and cook in the centre of the oven for about 20 minutes until a rich golden brown. Serve with a green salad.

TURKEY AU GRATIN WITH ALMONDS
Serves 6

This is one easy way to make your scraps of cold turkey into a deliciously satisfying hot dish. You can make it in a quiet moment and reheat it, or you can keep it hot in a low oven for hours.

For the meat
approx. 2 lb (800 g) cooked, boneless turkey
4 oz (100 g) blanched almonds – whole or split
1 oz (25 g) butter or margarine

For the sauce
2–3 oz (50–75 g) butter or margarine
2 heaped tablespoons (2 × 15 ml spoon) plain flour
1¼ pts (625 ml) milk

½ small glass sherry
6 oz (150 g) grated cheese
2 large cloves garlic – crushed
a little grated parmesan cheese
salt, black pepper
chopped parsley for decoration

Heat the oven to Gas Mark 3/325°F/160°C. Cut the turkey into pieces and arrange in a large, fairly shallow, oven-proof dish. Melt the 1 oz (25 g) butter in a frying pan and toss the almonds in it for a minute or two until golden brown. Sprinkle them over the cold turkey.
To make the sauce, melt the butter in a fairly large saucepan, take off the heat and stir in the flour with a wooden spoon. Gradually stir in the milk and bring to the boil, stirring all the time until it is a thick and smooth white sauce. Let it simmer, still stirring, for 2–3 minutes.

Then add the sherry, grated cheese, garlic, salt and black pepper and stir until the cheese has melted.

Pour the sauce over the turkey and almonds. Dot with butter and sprinkle with the grated parmesan. Cook in the centre of the oven for 30–45 minutes until golden brown.

Before serving, sprinkle chopped parsley round the edges of the dish. Serve with a salad.

GLAZED GOOSE WITH APPLES, GINGER AND GREEN CHILLIES

Serves 12–15

Few dishes seem more festive than a roasted goose. This recipe is not a traditional one but the combination of the rich, dark meet and the piquant apple mixture, rather like a fresh-flavoured apple curry, is quite delicious and easy to do. Allow at least 12 oz (375 g) of goose per person.

12–15 lb (5.4–6.7 kg) goose
4 oz (125 g) crystallized ginger
4 large garlic cloves
1–2-inch (2.5–5 cm) piece of fresh ginger, peeled
2 fresh green chillies, de-seeded
1½ lb (750 g) eating apple
juice of 1 lemon
6 tablespoons (6 x 15 ml spoons) natural yogurt
5 fl oz (150 ml) apple juice
2 tablespoons (2 x 15 ml spoons) caster sugar
2 tablespoons (2 x 15 ml spoons) dark soy sauce
a handful of chopped coriander, mint or parsley
salt, black pepper

Remove the giblets and remove and reserve any lumps of fat from the goose. Rub the skin with salt and put the goose breast-side down on a rack in a large roasting pan or dish. Place the pieces of goose fat on top and cover the dish with foil. Heat the oven to Gas Mark 4/350°F/180°C and cook the goose for 20 minutes per 1 lb (500 g).

While the goose is cooking, put the crystallized ginger in a small bowl of hot water and leave it to soak. Chop the peeled garlic, fresh ginger and chillies together finely. Peel, core and slice the apples. Take 4–5 tablespoons of goose fat from the roasting pan and heat this to medium heat in a flameproof casserole dish or heavy saucepan. Add the chopped garlic, fresh ginger and chillies and stir for 30 seconds. Add the sliced apples, stir and then cover the dish. Strain the soaked crystallized ginger and cut it into slivers. Add it to the cooked mixture, together with the lemon juice, and season with salt. Cover the pan again and cook over a low heat for 20–25 minutes, until the apples are fairly mushy. Stir in the yogurt and remove the pan from the heat.

About 45 minutes before the goose is finished cooking, pour out as much fat as possible from the pan and pour in the apple juice. Turn the goose over so that it is breast side-up. Stir the caster sugar into the soy sauce and brush the mixture all over the goose. Put it back in the oven without any foil.

When ready to serve, re-heat the apple mixture gently and stir in the chopped coriander, mint or parsley. Pour off any more fat from the pan juices; then season them to taste and use as gravy. The apple mixture should be spooned on top of the carved goose on your plate.

MALLARDS WITH SWEET ONION COMPOTE
Serves 6

Mallard, or wild duck, are completely different from commercially bred ducks. They have much darker, gamier flesh and are less fatty. Although they are not an economical buy, I snap them up whenever I see them in shops because they taste so good. For a meal over the Christmas season when there aren't too many of you, mallard make a real treat. I usually serve duck with brown rice and a crisp green vegetable; or for this dish a simple green salad is good.

> *2 oranges*
> *2 mallards, weighing about 1½–2 lb*
> *   (750–1 kg) each*
> *olive oil*
> *salt*

For the compote
1½ lb (750 g) small onions
2 oz (50 g) butter
1 tablespoon (15 ml spoon) olive oil
2 oz (50 g) walnuts, chopped roughly
1 oz (25 g) currants
1 oz (25 g) sultanas
2 teaspoons (2 x 5 ml spoons) bottled
*   green peppercorns*

2 teaspoons (2 x 5 ml spoons) ground
ginger
2 teaspoons (2 x 5 ml spoons) paprika
½ teaspoon (2.5 ml spoon) ground
cloves
2 rounded teaspoons (2 x 5 ml rounded
spoons) whole-seed mustard
2 tablespoons (2 x 15 ml spoons)
coarse-cut marmalade
1 tablespoon (15 ml spoon) red wine
vinegar
sea salt

For the Sauce

4 fl oz (125 ml) red wine
4 fl oz (125 ml) water
1 tablespoon (15 ml spoon) dark soy
sauce
sea salt, black pepper

Heat the oven to Gas Mark 6/400°F/200°C.
Put half of one orange into the body cavity of
each duck. Rub the outside with a little olive
oil and salt and put towards the top of the
oven, basting often, for 40 minutes.

While the ducks are cooking, make the
compote. Peel the onions and cut them
in quarters. Melt the butter with the oil in a
heavy-based saucepan over a medium heat.
Add the onions, the walnuts, the currants,
sultanas and the green peppercorns. Cover

the pan and cook, stirring occasionally,
for about 20 minutes until the onions are
completely soft. Then stir in the ground
ginger, paprika, cloves, the mustard, the
marmalade and the red wine vinegar.
Sprinkle with sea salt and return to the heat
for another 5 minutes.

When the mallards are cooked hold them
upside-down for any juices to pour out of
them into the roasting pan and then put the
ducks on a carving board. Pour most of the
fat from the pan. Add the juice of the second
orange to the pan with the red wine, the
water and the soy sauce. Season with black
pepper and salt and let it bubble fiercely in
the pan on top of the stove for 2–3 minutes.
Pour into a gravy jug and spoon the onion
compote into a warmed serving bowl to
accompany the duck.

GOLDEN DUCK WITH LYCHEE SAUCE
Serves 4–5

Cooking what is the most prized bird in China would seem to call for Chinese accompaniments. Simple to achieve, this dish is nevertheless just right to give a novel slant to a festive occasion. Both the texture and flavour of the sauce go beautifully with the duck, which should not be overcooked but remain slightly pink-fleshed. Serve it with either new potatoes or brown rice, and with mangetout peas or sliced and steamed Chinese leaves dotted with butter and sprinkled with soy sauce.

1 tablespoon (15 ml spoon) caster sugar
1 teaspoon (5 ml spoon) salt
4¾–5 lb (2.1–2.25 kg) duck
1 small onion
juice of 1 orange

For the sauce

11 oz (325 g) can of lychees
1 tablespoon (15 ml spoon) cornflour
6 tablespoons (6 x 15 ml spoons) water
2 tablespoons (2 x 15 ml spoons) dry
    sherry
a bunch of spring onions, chopped finely
cayenne pepper (chilli powder)
salt

Mix the sugar with the salt and rub the mixture all over the duck. Peel and coarsely chop the onion and put it in the body cavity of the duck, with a sprinkling of salt. Pour the orange juice into the body cavity and then skewer up the opening to enclose it. Put the duck on a rack in a roasting pan. Heat the oven to Gas Mark 4/350°F/180°C. Cook the duck in the centre of the oven for 40–45 minutes. Then turn the heat up to Gas Mark 9/475°F/240°C for another 10 minutes or so until the duck is richly brown and crisp.

While the duck is cooking, get ready to make the sauce. Strain the juice from the lychees into a small saucepan and leave on one side. Cut each lychee in half. Blend the cornflour in two tablespoons of the water. When the duck is ready take out the skewers, hold the duck with a cloth and pour the juices from inside it into the saucepan containing the lychee juice. Put the duck back in the roasting tin while you make the sauce.

Add the remaining four tablespoons of water and the sherry to the pan of juices. Stir in the blended cornflour and bring to the boil, stirring until the sauce thickens. Add the lychees and the chopped spring onions and boil again for another minute or so. Season to taste with salt and cayenne pepper (chilli powder). If the sauce seems too thick (this will depend on how much juice came out of the duck) stir in a little more water. Pour the sauce into a jug and serve separately.

OLD ENGLISH SPICED PHEASANTS WITH ONIONS AND WALNUTS
Serves 10

People are always asking me for different ways to cook pheasant. I created this dish for an old friend's seventieth birthday party. Spices go well with game and this combination of spices, onions, prunes and walnuts is particularly good; if you can use sweet red onions, all the better. You can increase the quantities for a buffet party. A red cabbage make a good accompaniment.

2 teaspoons (2 x 5 ml spoons) black peppercorns
2 teaspoons (2 x 5 ml spoons) allspice berries
1 teaspoon (5 ml spoon) cloves
1 teaspoon (5 ml spoon) mace blades
1 tablespoon (15 ml spoon) caster sugar
2 tablespoons (2 x 15 ml spoons) red wine vinegar
1 tablespoon (15 ml spoon) olive or sunflower oil
2 large pheasants
1½ lb (750 g) onions, sliced in rings
4 oz (125 g) walnut pieces
4 oz (125 g) pitted prunes, quartered
6–7 fl oz (175–210 ml) dry sherry or cider
butter

In a coffee grinder, or using a pestle and motar, grind up the peppercorns and spices. Mix them in a bowl with the caster sugar, the vinegar and the oil. Smear this mixture all over the pheasants. Put them in a large roasting pan, cover them with foil and leave in a cool place or the fridge for several hours or overnight.

Spread the onion rings over the bottom of the roasting pan; add the pheasants, together with the walnut pieces, quartered prunes and sherry or cider. Dot generously with butter and cover the dish with foil. Heat the oven to Gas Mark 5/375°F/190°C. Cook in the centre of the oven for 1½ –1¾ hours. Remove the foil from the dish for the last 15 minutes of cooking time. Serve the onion mixture and juices in a bowl to spoon over the individual plates of carved pheasant; or for easier serving at a buffet party you can mix the carved slices with the onion mixture and serve together in a large, open serving dish.

HUMBLE PIE
Serves 6

In our house Christmas Eve is for last-minute preparations and wrapping up of stocking presents. It is also the day before the big meal, so I always feel that supper on Christmas Eve should be something homely and satisfying, not rich and lavish, in view of what is to follow. So I suggest this layered pie, a very popular family dish. It makes a busy evening simpler because it can be prepared beforehand and then just put in the oven and it only needs a green salad as an accompaniment.

2½ lb (1.1 kg) swede
1 lb (500 g) leeks
2 large garlic cloves
2 tablespoons (2 x 15 ml spoon) olive oil
2 lb (1 kg) lean minced pork
2 teaspoons (2 x 5 ml spoons) dill seeds
1 tablespoon (15 ml spoon) tomato purée
1 tablespoon (15 ml spoon) thick honey
juice of 1 lemon
2 oz (50 g) butter
8–10 oz (250–300 g) Jerusalem
    artichokes
2 oz (50 g) Gruyère cheese, grated
salt, black pepper

Peel the swede, chop it roughly and steam or boil it until soft. Meanwhile, trim and wash the leeks and cut them across in rings. Peel the garlic and chop it finely. Heat the olive oil over a high heat in a wide saucepan or large, deep frying-pan. Add the minced pork. Break it up while it cooks and continue until the juices have evaporated. Add the chopped garlic, the dill seeds, the tomato purée, the honey and the lemon juice. Stir in thoroughly; then add the chopped leeks and stir over the heat until just softened. Season well with salt and black pepper. Spoon into a round, open ovenproof dish and smooth the top.

Mash the swede, mash in the butter and season with salt and plenty of black pepper. Spread the mashed swede evenly over the meat mixture. Lastly wash the jerusalem artichokes well but leave them unpeeled; slice them thinly and arrange the slices neatly in a single layer on top of the swede. Scatter the grated cheese over the artichokes. When ready to cook the pie, heat the oven to Gas Mark 4/350°F/180°C and cook in the centre for about 45 minutes.

ROAST BEEF STUFFED WITH SMOKED OYSTERS WITH CUCUMBER SAUCE
Serves about 8

There are some recipes that I could not be more pleased with. This is one of them, a real treat which requires very little effort. The marriage of beef and smoked oysters is an inexplicable success. The oysters are mixed with parsley and onion and the smoky taste permeates the roast beef to give an ambrosial flavour. The light, refreshing sauce perfects the pleasure of the dish. Serve with roast potatoes, and a green vegetable or braised chicory.

3½ oz (105 g) can of smoked oysters, drained
a large bunch of parsley, chopped finely
1 small onion, chopped finely
3 lb (1.25 kg) joint of beef
olive oil
sea salt, black pepper

For the Sauce
½ cucumber, peeled and chopped finely
3 tablespoons (3 x 15 ml spoons) natural yogurt
2 teaspoons (2 x 5 ml spoons) lemon juice

5 fl oz (150 ml) carton of double cream
2–3 pinches of cayenne pepper (chilli powder)
salt

Put the oysters in a bowl, mix them with the chopped parsley and onion and season with plenty of black pepper. Cut any string from the joint of beef and then press the oyster mixture into the cavaties. Tie the joint up neatly again with string and rub it all over with olive oil. Rub the outer fat with sea salt. Put the meat in a roasting tin and leave it for 3–4 hours at room temperature.

Preheat the oven to Gas Mark 7/425°F/220°C and cook the beef towards the top of the oven, basting it once or twice, for 10–15 minutes per 1 lb (500 g) to give rare beef, or 20–30 minutes for medium to well done meat.

To make the sauce, put the chopped cucumber in a bowl and mix in the yogurt and lemon juice. Season with a little salt and the cayenne pepper (chilli powder). Whisk the cream until thick and fold gently into the cucumber mixture. Pour into a serving bowl and keep in the fridge until ready to serve with the cooked beef.

HARE IN A RICH AND SHINY SAUCE
Serves 10

Hare has a wonderfully full flavour which we taste all too rarely. I first made this delicious dish for New Year's Eve. It is perfect to sustain you for the long night ahead. You can cook hare well beforehand and finish the sauce in a few minutes before you eat. I cook red cabbage in a casserole to go with this and then stir some briefly steamed broccoli into it at the last moment. Brown rice goes well with the sauce.

½ pint (300 ml) + 2 tablespoons (2 x 15 ml spoons) hot water
1 oz (25 g) dried mushrooms
2 tablespoons (2 x 15 ml spoons) sunflower oil
10 good-sized joints of hare
2 large onions
8 oz (250 g) carrots
coarsely grated rind and juice of 1 orange
3 teaspoons (3 x 5 ml spoons) dried green peppercorns
2 teaspoons (2 x 5 ml spoons) ground mace
3 large garlic cloves, peeled and chopped finely
1 tablespoon (15 ml spoon) thick honey
6 fl oz (175 ml) red wine
2 tabespoons (2 x 15 ml spoons) arrowroot
chopped parsley
salt

Pour ½ pint (300 ml) very hot water over the dried mushrooms in a bowls and leave them to soak while you prepare the rest of the ingredients. Heat the sunflower oil in a large frying-pan over a high heat. Add as many joints of hare as will fit in the pan and just brown them on each side. Transfer the joints to a large, heavy saucepan, and then repeat with the remaining joints. Peel the onion, chop them roughly and put them in a food processor with the carrots, also roughly chopped. Whizz until they have turned to a mush. Turn into a bowl and stir in the orange rind and juice, the mushrooms and their soaking water, the green peppercorns, the mace, the chopped garlic, the honey and the wine. Season with salt and pour the mixture over the joints in the saucepan. Cover the pan, bring it to the boil and then leave it to simmer gently for 1½–1¾ hours until the hare is very tender. Remove from the heat.

Before serving re-heat in the saucepan and then remove the joints with a slotted spatula and arrange in a large serving dish. Add the wine vinegar to the saucepan juices and

47

check for seasoning. Mix the arrowroot in a cup with the 2 tablespoons water until smooth. Stir the mixture into the saucepan juices and put over the heat. Bring to the boil stirring, and simmer, still stirring, for 3 minutes. Then pour over the hare joints and scatter with chopped parsley.

BOXING NIGHT BEEF

Serves 6

This rich and glossy casserole of beef and mushrooms cooked in a dark chestnut sauce doesn't have to be served on Boxing night, but by then you may have had two meals of cold bits and pieces and in my experience this kind of soothing, warming dish is just what people want after quite a lot of cold food. It is not just an ordinary stew and will seem quite festive enough for the occasion. The casserole can be made well ahead; dishes like this even seem to improve with re-heating. Small potatoes boiled in their skins go well with it and a mixture of broccoli and finely sliced red cabbage.

2 large onions
4 tablespoons (4 x 15 ml spoons) olive oil
2½ lb (1.1 kg) lean braising steak, cubed
3 bay leaves

15 oz (450 g) can of unsweetened chestnut purée
1 level tablespoon (15 ml level spoon) black treacle
2 teaspoons (2 x 5 ml spoons) paprika
¾ pint (450 ml) beef stock
12 oz (375 g) medium-sized mushrooms, halved
5 rounded tablespoons (5 x rounded 15 ml spoons) fromage frais or greek yogurt
4 teaspoons (4 x 5 ml spoons) whole-seed mustard
salt, black pepper

Peel the onions, cut in half and slice thinly. Heat 3 tablespoons of the olive oil in a large frying-pan over a low to medium heat. Add the onions and cook, stirring around often until softened and slightly browned at the edges. Remove the pan from the heat and, using a slotted spoon, transfer the onions to a plate on one side. Sprinkle the beef lightly all over with salt. Heat the remaining tablespoon of olive oil in the frying-pan over a high heat. Add the pieces of meat (you will probably have to do this in several batches, adding a little more oil if necessary) and turn around to brown on all sides. Then remove them with a slotted spoon and put them in a flameproof casserole.

Add the onions and bay leaves. Spoon the chestnut purée into a food processor with the black treacle, the paprika, plenty of black pepper and the beef stock. Whizz until smooth and then pour it over the beef and onions. Heat the oven to Gas Mark 2/300°F/150°C. Cover the casserole and bring the sauce to bubbling on top of the stove; the cook just below the centre of the oven for 2 hours.

Add the mushrooms, and return to the oven, turning down the heat to Gas Mark 1/275°/140°C. Continue cooking for another hour or so until the beef is very tender. Meanwhile, put the fromage frais or yogurt into a bowl and stir in the mustard. Before serving the casserole spoon the fromage frais or yogurt on top of it; it will mix in roughly as you serve it out.

SPICED BEEF AND CHESTNUT PIE
Serves 8

There is something about the appearance of a pie, with its cheering, golden glow, that always suits a special occasion. Pies are also useful for parties because they can be prepared in advance and kept warm in the oven for some time without spoiling. And everyone seems to like them! This one, with its rich and crumbly pastry, is perfect for a Christmas celebration. You can serve it with just one green vegetable or simply a salad.

For the filling
1 oz (25 g) butter
2 large onions, sliced coarsely
2 lb (1 kg) braising steak, cut into 1–2-inch (2.5–5 cm) chunks
1 heaped teaspoon (5 ml heaped spoon) ground allspice
1 teaspoon (5 ml spoon) juniper berries, crushed coarsely
2 teaspoons (2 x 5 ml spoons) bottled green peppercorns
1 tablespoon (15 ml spoon) caster sugar
¼ pint (150 m) red wine
10 oz (300 g) canned whole chestnuts, drained
salt, black pepper

For the Pastry

8 oz (250 g) plain flour
½ teaspoon (2.5 ml spoon) salt
3 oz (75 g) lard
3 0z (75 g) frozen butter
1 egg, whisked
1 tablespoon (15 ml spoon) cold water
milk or egg yolk, to glaze

Heat the butter in a flameproof casserole or heavy based frying-pan and fry the onions over a medium to high heat until soft and brown. Using s slotted spatula, transfer the onions to a plate on one side. Then add the braising steak and fry over a high heat, stirring, until sealed all over. Add the allspice and after a minute remove it from the heat. Heat the oven to Gas Mark 2/300°F/150°C. Return the onion to the pan and add the crushed juniper berries and green peppercorns. Season with salt, a very little black pepper and the caster sugar. Pour in the wine. Return to the heat and bring to the boil. Transfer to a casserole, if using a frying-pan. Cover and put in the centre of the oven for 1½–2 hours.

While the meat is cooking make the pastry. Sift the flour and salt in a bowl and rub in the lard with your fingertips until it is like fine breadcrumbs. Coarsely grate the frozen butter and add it to the flour, mixing it in lightly with a knife. Then add the whisked egg and the cold water and mix it with a knife until the dough begins to stick together. Press lightly into a ball, wrap in cling film and put in the fridge.

When the meat is tender, gently stir in the chestnuts, transfer the mixture to a 2½-pint (1.5-litre) pie dish and leave until cold. Then take the pastry from the fridge and knead it slightly to make it manageable. Take off a piece of dough and form it with your hands into a long strip to put around the rim of the pie dish. Moisten the rim and put the strip in position. Roll out the remaining pastry into a piece just big enough to top the pie dish. Press the edges together lightly and trim them neatly all round . Roll out the trimmings and cut out decorations. Cut two small holes in the top of the pie for steam to escape. If there is time, put the pie in the fridge for 30 minutes or more before cooking.

Heat the oven to Gas Mark 7/425°F/220°C. Brush the pie with milk or egg yolk for a really golden glaze and bake it in the centre of the oven for 20 minutes; then turn down the heat to Gas Mark 4/350°C/180°C and bake it for another 15–20 minutes.

SPICED CRISPY PIGEON PIE
Serves 10

This delectable party pie can be made well in advance and then served hot, with just a mixed salad and good bread. The full flavour of pigeon goes beautifully with the fresh ginger and spring onion and the paper-thin fillo or strudel pastry makes it something very special.

8 wood pigeons
2 sticks of cinnamon, broken into 1-inch
(2.5 cm) pieces
2 teaspoons (2 x 5 ml spoons) paprika
¾ pint (450 ml) water
1 tablespoon (15 ml spoon) caster sugar
2-inch (5 cm) piece of fresh ginger,
peeled and chopped finely
3 large garlic cloves, peeled and
chopped finely
finely grated find of ½ lemon
2 bunches of spring onions
4 oz (125 g) butter
12 oz (375 g) fillo pastry
salt, black pepper

Put the pigeons in a large, heavy saucepan. Intersperse the broken sticks of cinnamon and sprinkle on the paprika and salt and pepper. Add the water. Cover the pan and bring to the boil; then turn down the heat and simmer very gently for about 2 hours until the pigeons are tender. When the pigeons are cool enough to handle, cut and pick all the flesh off them (cutting up any large pieces) and put into a large bowl.

Strain off the pan juices into a smaller saucepan and stir in the caster sugar. Boil over a fierce heat for 7–10 minutes until well reduced and syrupy. Stir in the chopped ginger and garlic and the grated lemon rind. Pour the reduced juices on to the pigeon flesh and mix well. Peel the spring onions and chop them, using as much of the green stalk as possible, and mix them in with the pigeons. Season with salt and pepper if necessary.

Melt the butter in a mall saucepan and brush a very large round or square ovenproof dish with some of it. Lay a sheet of fillo pastry on the dish, folding in the edges to fit, and brush it thinly with butter. Then lay on a second sheet. Spoon in the pigeon mixture. Lay another sheet of pastry on top, again folding in the edges, brush with butter and continue like this in layers until all the pastry is used up, brushing the top sheet of pastry with butter, too. You can now cook the pie at once if you like or keep it until later. Once cooked it will keep well for some time in a low oven.

Heat the oven to Gas Mark 3/325°F/170°C and cook the pie in the centre for 30–40 minutes; then increase the heat to Gas Mark 8/450°F/230°C, just for 5–10 minutes, until the pastry is a rich golden-brown.

ROAST SADDLE OF LAMB WITH THYME AND MUSTARD SAUCE

Serves 8–12

If you want a change from roast beef or pork over Christmas you might treat yourself to a saddle of lamb. A saddle is a magnificent looking joint and will feed 8–12 people depending on its size. Carve the meat in long, thin strips down the length of the joint.

juice of 1 lemon
4 tablespoons (4 x 15 ml spoons) olive oil, plus extra
2 garlic cloves, chopped finely
a saddle of English lamb
2 tablespoons (2 x 15 ml spoons) fresh thyme leaves
salt, black pepper

For the sauce
1 oz (25 g) butter
1 oz (25 g) cornflour
½ pint (300 ml) milk
1 rounded tablespoon (15 ml spoon)

fresh thyme leaves
2 rounded teaspoons (2 x 5 ml spoons) whole-seed mustard
2–3 pinches of cayenne pepper (chilli powder)
salt

If possible, prepare the joint the night before. Mix the lemon juice in a bowl with the olive oil an chopped garlic and season with salt an black pepper. Rub the lamb all over with this mixture. Sprinkle the thyme on the underside of the meat and press it into any cracks. Leave the joint underside up so that the thyme stays on the flesh. Cover the pan and leave in a cool room for several hours or overnight.

Hear the oven to Gas Mark 4/350°F/180°C. Turn the joint over in the pan and smear the fat with a little more olive oil and salt. Roast in the centre of the oven for 15–25 minutes per pound, basting occasionally.

When the lamb is nearly ready start making the sauce. Melt the butter in a saucepan. Remove from the hear and blend in the cornflour. Gradually stir in the milk and bring to the boil, stirring. Simmer gently, still stirring, for 2–3 minutes. Stir in the thyme and mustard. Remove the lamb to a carving board and pour away the excess fat from the pan. Add the remaining pan juices to the sauce. Lastly season to taste with cayenne pepper (chilli powder) and sale and serve in a sauce boat to accompany the meat.

FESTIVE PHEASANTS

Serves 16-18

Here is a delectable dish for a big dinner or Christmas lunch party. If possible try to seat everyone: food is so much more enjoyable when you don't have to stand balancing your plate precariously, unable to concentrate properly either on eating or taking. In this recipe, which has a mild Anglo-Indian flavour, pheasant joints are marinated with yogurt and spices to a mouthwatering tenderness. The creamy, aromatic sauce goes perfectly with a large bowl of Indian basmati rice. Other than that I just serve a salad so it is an easy meal to prepare and serve despite the large quantity. To those who say that pheasants are dull birds I can only reply that this way of cooking them may change their minds. If you are worried about cutting the pheasants into smallish joints I find it very easy if I use a large, sharp knife and then a hammer to bang it through the bird. Noisy but effective! You do need to start this recipe 2–3 day before you want to serve it.

4 pheasants
3-inch (7.5 cm) piece of fresh ginger
4-5 large garlic cloves
3-4 green chillies
8 oz (250 g) natural yogurt
1 teaspoon (5 ml spoon) ground cloves
2 teaspoons (2 x 5 ml spoons) ground cinnamon
juice of 1 lemon
2 tablespoons (2 x 15 ml spoons) white wine vinegar
4 tablespoons (4 x 15 ml spoons) tomato purée
1 tablespoon (15 ml spoon) black onion seed, if available
¾ pint (450 ml) double cream
a bunch of fresh coriander leaves
sea salt

Joint the pheasants: I like to make six joints of each bird. Cut them in half first and then cut off the legs. Divide the remaining pieces in half. Put them into a very large casserole dish (or use a jam-making pan that has a lid). Peel the ginger and garlic and chop them together finely. Cut open the chillies under running water, discard the seeds and then chop the flesh finely. In a mixing bowl put the yogurt, the ground spices, the lemon juice, the vinegar and the tomato purée. Add the chopped ginger, garlic and chillies and the black onion seeds if using them. Mix thoroughly and then add the mixture to the dish of pheasants and smear well onto each joint (it is best to do this with your hands, though messy). Cover the dish and leave in a cool place until next day or even the day after, turning the joints around in the marinade two or three times.

Heat the oven to Gas Mark 9/475°F/240°C. Put the covered dish in the oven for 1¼–1½ hours. Have one very large or two smaller, wide, fairly shallow dishes ready and warmed. Using a slotted spatula, remove the pieces of pheasant and arrange them on the serving dishes. Pour off some of the fat from the casserole and then pour the cream into the cooking juices. Stir, bring to the boil and simmer, stirring for 2–3 minutes. Remove from the heat and add salt to taste. Pull the leaves off the coriander stems. Before serving spoon the cream sauce over the pheasants joints and sprinkle with coriander leaves all over.

ROAST LEG OF LAMB SPIKED WITH PEARS AND ROSEMARY
Serves 6

Generations of British cooks have ruined leg of lamb by overcooking it. It is a lean joint and if cooked until brown all through the meat loses both succulence and flavour. In France they often cook lamb leaving it almost red inside but I like it best a delicate pink. Lamb responds well when cooked with fruit; particularly, I have discovered, with pears. This is an easy dish to prepare and would do well for either Christmas Eve or Boxing Day. Sliced potatoes, cooked in a dish with garlic and cream, go beautifully with this roast. Perry is a drink like cider made from pears; cider does just as well.

4½–5 lb (2–2.25 kg) leg of lamb
4–6 sprigs of fresh rosemary
grated rind and juice of 1 lemon
12 oz (375 g) firm but not hard pears
olive oil
½ pint (300 ml) cider or perry
5 fl oz (150 ml) carton of double cream
*   (optional)*
sea salt, black pepper

Using a very sharp knife make deep cuts about ¾ inch (2 cm) apart all along the back of the leg of lamb. Insert the leaves from the rosemary sprigs and the grated lemon rind. Peel and core the pears, slice them thinly and insert the slices right into the meat, filling the incisions. Lay the leg cut-side up in a roasting pan. Pour the lemon juice into the incisions and sprinkle the leg generously all over with black pepper. Cover the pan with cling film and leave at room temperature for 2 hours or so (or put in the fridge overnight), spooning the juices over it now and then.

Before cooking it, turn the lamb over in the pan skin-side up and rub the skin with sea salt and olive oil. Heat the oven to Gas Mark 8/450°F/230°C and roast the lamb in the centre for 10 minutes; then turn down the heat to Gas Mark 5/375°F/190°C, add the cider or perry and cook for another 50–60 minutes depending on the weight of the leg. Baste frequently with the juices.

When cooked, remove the lamb from the oven and let it sit on top of the stove for 10–15 minutes before eating. Check the pan juices for seasoning and re-heat before pouring into the gravy jug. To make the gravy into more of a sauce add the double cream to the juices in the pan and simmer them on top of the stove for a minute or two.

STEAMED CHICKEN PUDDING WITH CHICORY, LEMON AND GINGER
Serves 6

Although Christmas is a time for traditional dishes sometimes I cannot resist giving them an exciting twist. What could be more old-fashioned and English than a steamed pudding presented in its basin, wrapped in a white linen napkin? The light crust of this pudding is made with butter instead of suet; it is spiced and full of taste. Once broken into, the crust reveals not steak and kidney but a filling of lemony chicken with chicory which is mouthwatering and delicate. I serve this pudding simply with a green salad or green beans.

> 2 lb (1 kg) boned and skinned chicken
>   (breast, thigh or both)
> l oz (25 g) plain flour, plus extra for rolling
> 2 tablespoons (2 x 15 ml spoons) olive oil
> 6 oz (175 g) self-raising flour
> 3 teaspoons (3 x 5 ml spoons) paprika
> 1 teaspoon (5 ml spoon) ground mace
> 2 teaspoons (2 x 5 ml spoons) dried dill
> 3–4 good pinches cayenne pepper (chilli
>   powder)
> 4 oz (125 g) fresh white breadcrumbs
> 6 oz (175 g) frozen butter, plus extra for
>   greasing
> 1 egg

water
2-inch (5 cm) piece of fresh ginger
2 large garlic cloves
3 heads of chicory
coarsely grated rind and juice of 1 lemon
salt, black pepper

Cut the chicken into largish chunks. Put the plain flour into a bowl and season it with salt and black pepper. Add the chicken and turn it around to coat it with flour. Heat the olive oil in a large frying-pan over a high heat. Add the chicken pieces and fry just to brown them on all sides; then remove from the heat and leave in a bowl on one side to cool.

Put the self-raising flour in a bowl and mix in the spices, the dill, the cayenne pepper (chilli powder) and salt. Stir in the breadcrumbs. Holding the frozen butter in a cloth at one end, coarsely grate it into the flour and breadcrumb mixture, mixing it in lightly with your fingertips. Whisk the egg lightly in a measuring jug and bring it up to 6fl oz (175 ml) with water. Gradually stir the liquid into the flour mixture. Bring together and form a ball. Cut off a little over a quarter of the dough for the lid. Roll out the large piece of dough fairly thinly on a floured board into a large circle 13–14 inches (33–36 cm) across. Butter a 3-pint (1.75-litre) pudding basin. Carefully lift the large piece of pastry and line the basin,

pressing it together if it tears and leaving the excess hanging over the edge.

Put a large saucepan half full of water on to boil. Peel the ginger and garlic and chip finely. Cut the chicory across in thickish slices. Mix the chopped ginger and garlic, the lemon rind and the sliced chicory with the browned chicken. Add the lemon juice and season with salt and black pepper. Spoon the mixture into the lined basin, piling it up in a mound at the top. Fold the overlapping pasty over the filling and dampen the folded-over edges. Roll out the reserved dough in a circle big enough for the top. Press the edges lightly to seal them. Butter a piece of greaseproof paper, make a pleat in the middle and put it over the top of the pudding. Put a piece of foil fairly loosely over the paper and tie both securely round the basin with string. Make a string handle and then lower the basin into the saucepan of boiling water. Cover and boil gently for 3–3½ hours (or 1 hour in a pressure cooker) topping up the water now and then so that it doesn't boil away.

WISE MEN'S PIE
Serves 6

After Boxing Day is over I begin to want hot food again and by then fish seems preferable to meat, but the shops are often still closed. Frozen fish can be dull, but one fish which loses nothing with freezing – in fact many people feel it improves in texture – is squid. So if you put some in your freezer before Christmas you can make this very delicious and different kind of fish pie which we will be most refreshing after all the rich food and cold meats.

a pinch of saffron strands
½ pint (300 ml) milk
2 lb (1 kg) squid, thawed if frozen
1 large onion
1 large red pepper
4 oz (125 g) mushrooms
4 oz (125 g) butter
1 oz (25 g) plain flour
1 tablespoon (15 ml spoon) lemon juice
2½ lb (1.1 kg) large potatoes
a little cream or top of the milk
salt, black pepper

Put the saffron strands in a small saucepan with the milk and bring to the boil. Remove from the heat, stir round, cover the pan and leave on one side. Prepare the squid

by pulling off the head and tentacles and then discarding the head and black eyes but keeping the tentacles and the main body of the squid. Then press out the soft, white innards of the squid and pull out the transparent plastic-like bone. This may all seem a bit strange at first but is easy to do. Then cut the squid across into ½-inch (1 cm) rings and put these into a sieve over a bowl on one side.

Peel the onion, halve it and slice it fairly thinly in half circles. Cut the pepper in half, discard the seeds and slice it fairly thinly. Slice the mushrooms across in medium thick slices. Melt half the butter in a large, deep frying-pan over a medium heat. Add the sliced onions and peppers and cook, stirring often, until really soft and slightly browned at the edges. Remove from the heat and stir in the flour. Gradually stir in the saffron milk, return to the heat and just bubble, stirring for a minute or two until thickened. Add the mushrooms and squid and stif over the heat for 4–5 minutes, just until the squid has turned opaque. Remove from the heat, stir in the lemon juice, season with salt and black pepper and turn the mixture into a fairly shallow ovenproof dish.

Peel the potatoes, quarter them and boil or steam until cooker. Mash with the remaining butter and a little cream on top of the milk. Season with salt and black pepper. Spread the potato evenly on top of the squid mixture and criss-cross it in a pattern with a fork.

Heat the oven to Gas Mark 9/475°F/240°C. Put the pie in at the very top for about 15 minutes until the potato is speckled brown on top.

PIGEONS WITH A COMPOTE OF RED CABBAGE
Serves 4

I always think of this as a New Year's dish. It's a simple pigeon casserole which can be made ahead and re-heats well. This is one of those dishes which are particularly heartening on a cold day, and the temperature usually seems to drop once the excitement of Christmas Day has passed.

> 2 rounded tablespoons (2 x 15 ml rounded spoons) plain flour
> 4 wood pigeons
> 2 tablespoons (2 x 15 ml spoons) sunflower oil, plus extra if necessary
> 4 table spoons (4 x 15 ml spoons) olive oil
> salt, black pepper

For the compote
2 largish onions
2 oz (50 g) butter
1 lb (500 g) red cabbage
2-inch (5 cm) piece of fresh ginger
2 large garlic cloves
2 teaspoons (2 x 5 ml spoons) caraway seeds
4 oz (125 g) pitted prunes, cut in half
¼ pint (150 ml) red wine
salt

First make the compote. Peel the onions and chop them roughly. Melt the butter in a large flameproof casserole over a medium heat, add the onion and cook until soft and just beginning to brown. Meanwhile chop up the red cabbage finely. Peel the ginger and the garlic and chop them together finely. When the onion is soft add the chopped ginger and garlic followed by the cabbage. Add the caraway seeds, the halved prunes and the wine. Season with salt. Cover the casserole dish with a lid and remove it from the heat.

Put the flour into a bowl and season with salt and black pepper. Dip the pigeons in the flour to coat them thoroughly. Heat the sunflower oil in a large frying-pan over a high heat and try the pigeons just to brown them on all sides, adding more oil if necessary. Arrange them on top of the red cabbage and spoon a tablespoon of olive oil over each one. Heat the oven to Gas Mark 3/325°F/170°C. Cook, covered in the centre of the oven for about 1½ hours.

MARINATED AND SPIKED ROAST LEG OF PORK

Serves 12–15

Prepare the pork the night before so that it has time to absorb the flavours of the marinade. I think this flavourful joint is best with a simple apple sauce and gravy made from the juices.

1 leg of port
3 large garlic cloves
2-inch (5 cm) piece of fresh ginger
grated rind and juice of 2 oranges
3 tablespoons (3 x 15 ml spoons) whole-seed mustard
4 tablespoons (4 x 15 ml spoons) thick honey
3 teaspoons (3 x 5 ml spoons) ground coriander
1 teaspoon (5 ml spoon) ground cloves
oil
caster sugar
sea salt, black pepper

Line a roasting pan with a large piece of foil which comes a long way over the edges of the pan. Using a very sharp knife, score the skin of the pork in a criss-cross pattern all over. Then insert the knife into the flesh of the pork in several places to make pockets for flavourings. Put the leg on the foil in the roasting pan. Peel the garlic and ginger and chop them finely together. Mix them in a bowl with the grated orange rind and 1 tablespoon of the mustard. Now press this mixture into the deep incisions you have made in the pork flesh. Then mix the orange juice with the remaining mustard, the honey and the ground spices in another bowl. Season with plenty of black pepper and rub the mixture all over the joint but not on the hard skin. Bring the foil up all round the pork but leave the hard skin exposed. Leave in a cool place overnight.

When you are ready to cook the joint, heat the oven to Gas Mark 5/375°F/190°C. Smear the hard skin with oil and sprinkle if with caster sugar and sea salt. Cover the joint loosely with greaseproof paper, tucking it into the foil. Cover the shank (thin) end completely with foil, so it does not dry out. Put the pork into the centre of the oven for 25 minutes per pound plus 25 minutes, opening up the foil and removing the paper completely for the last 30 minutes or so. If the hard skin hasn't crisped you can turn up the oven to its highest setting for about 15 minutes at the end.

LAMB CRACKER

Serves 6–8

Paper-thin sheets of fillo pastry, which you buy ready to use, can be transformed miraculously into all sorts of impressive creations. At Christmas time what could be more appropriate than a large cracker tie with a bow? This one is filled with an exciting mixture of spiced lamb with pears and walnuts. The cracker can be made well ahead and is perfect for a Christmas dinner party. I serve it with a mixture of steamed carrots and leeks and if possible the yellow-fleshed, waxy new potatoes which you can often find during the winter, or Pink Fir Apple potatoes.

2 lb (1 kg) lamb neck fillets
½ teaspoon (2.5 ml spoon) cloves
1 teaspoon (5 ml spoon) allspice berries
1½ teaspoons (1½ x 5 ml spoon) dried
*   green peppercorns*
1 teaspoon (5 ml spoon) juniper berries
2 large garlic cloves

4 oz (125 g) dried pears
2 tablespoons (2 x 15 ml spoons)
*   sunflower oil*
6–8 strips orange peel
2 oz (50 g) walnuts, chopped roughly
13 oz (400 g) can of chopped tomatoes
2 oz (50 g) butter, plus extra for greasing
1 lb (500 g) fillo pastry
salt

Cut the lamb fillets into 1-inch (2.5 cm) pieces. Either in a coffee grinder or using a pestle and motar, grind together the cloves, the allspice and the green peppercorns. Roughly crush the juniper berries. Peel and finely chop the garlic. Cut the pears in half lengthways. Heat 1 tablespoon of oil in a heavy flameproof casserole over a medium heat, add the chopped garlic and the ground spices and stir for a minute. Add the juniper berries, the pears, the orange peel and the walnuts. Now add the chopped tomatoes and season with a little salt. Heat the oven to Gas Mark 2/300°F/150°C. Cover the casserole and bring it just to the boil on top of the stove; then put it in the centre of the oven for 1½–2 hours, stirring occasionally, until the lamb is very tender. Remove from the oven and leave until cold.

Gently melt the butter in a small saucepan and remove it from the heat. Lightly butter a large baking sheet. Lay a sheet of fillo pastry on it, brush the pastry with melted butter, lay another sheet, brush again with butter and so on until you have used all but two sheets of pastry. Now spoon the cold lamb filling in a piled-up strip lengthways along the centre of the pastry coming within about 3 inches (7.5 cm) of the pastry edges. Bring up the sides of the pastry to join, brushing one edge with butter and then pressing the edges to seal.

Turn the cracker carefully over and place it crossways on the buttered baking sheet. Pinch the ends where the meat ends to look like a cracker. Using a sharp knife, cut diagonal lines across the cracker. Brush one of the remaining fillo sheets with butter and put the other on top. Cut two 1-inch (2.5 cm) wide strips and arrange them gently around the two end of the cracker like tied bows. Fold over the remaining big piece of pasty and make into a large bow to put in the centre of the cracker. Finally, brush the whole cracker with melted butter.

Heat the oven to Gas Mark 6/400°F/200°C. Put the cracker in the centre of the oven for 20 minutes; then turn down the heat to Gas Mark 3/325°F/170°C and continue cooking for another 30-40 minutes until richly browned. Protect the ends of the cracker and the decorations with foil, if necessary, to stop them browning too quickly.

THE COLD TABLE AND SALADS

It is useful to have cold meat around over Christmas but it must be full of flavour to contrast with the blandness of the cold turkey. Good salads, also, are essential at Christmas to accompany cold meats and turkey or to go with ready-prepared hot dishes so that you won't have to be busy cooking vegetables at the last minute. I have included a few less usual salads which can be prepared and most of them dressed beforehand without losing their fresh appearance and taste.

"In a sallet every plant should come in to bear its part without being overpowered by some herb of a stronger taste, but fall into their places like the notes in music".

John Evelyn (1620–1706)

SWEET SPICED GAMMON

Serves 15–20

It is traditional to have a ham at Christmas and the way to ensure that it is full of flavour and character is to prepare and cook it yourself. In this recipe I bake the ham in the old fashioned way, encased in a flour and water paste. I think it tastes better like this but you can cook it wrapped in foil if you prefer.

approximately 11 lb (4.95 kg) smoked gammon on the bone
3 tablespoons (3 x 15 ml spoons) black treacle

2 tablespoons (2 x 15 ml spoons) dark brown sugar
3 teaspoons (3 x 5 ml spoons) black peppercorns
2 teaspoons (2 x 5 ml spoons) allspice berries
1 teaspoon (5 ml spoon) cloves
2–3 teaspoons (2–3 x 5 ml spoons) juniper berries
1½ lb (750 g) plain flour
water

For the glaze

3 teaspoons (3 x 5 ml spoon) French mustard
1 tablespoon (15 ml spoon) redcurrant jelly

Soak the gammon in a large sink of cold water, if possible, overnight, changing the water once or twice. Take it out and pat it dry. In a bowl, put the black treacle and the dark brown sugar. Grind the black peppercorns, the allspice and the cloves in a coffee grinder or with a pestle and motar. Mix them into the black treacle and sugar. Roughly crush the juniper berries and press them into any cracks in the gammon. Smear the treacle and spice mixture over the flesh.

Mix the flour with enough cold water to make an elastic dough. Roll the dough out on a floured board into a piece large enough to wrap up the gammon. Wrap it very loosely – since it shrinks while cooking – and press the edges to seal. Patch up any cracks or holes with foil. Put the parcel into a roasting pan join-sides uppermost. Heat the oven to Gas Mark 4/350°F/180°C, put the pan on a low shelf and bake for 20–25 minutes per 1 lb (500 g).

When the gammon is cooked, break off the flour crust and cut off the hard skin while it is still hot. Using a sharp knife cut a diamond pattern in the fat. Turn up the oven to Gas Mark 6/400°F/200°C. For the glaze, mix the mustard and redcurrant jelly in a bowl and then brush the mixture over the fat. Put the gammon back in the oven for 15–20 minutes until well glazed. Leave until cold.

TREACLE BAKED COLLAR OF BACON
Serves 8–12

This aromatic piece of meat will keep well, foil-wrapped in the fridge. It is ideal for a party or if you are feeding a lot of people over Christmas. You can cook any bacon or gammon joint in this way but collar is an economical cut. You can use smoked or green bacon, but I nearly always go for smoked meat because I prefer the flavour.

2½-3 lb (1–1.25 kg) piece of collar of bacon
¼ oz (½ × 2.5 ml spoon) allspice berries and ¼ oz cloves or just ½ oz (2.5 ml spoon) cloves
¼-½ oz (½-1 × 2.5 ml spoon) black peppercorns
black treacle
demerara sugar

Soak the bacon in cold water for at least 3 hours or overnight, changing the water once or twice, to remove excess saltiness. Put the spices and peppercorns into a liquidiser or coffee grinder and whizz up until roughly ground. Mix them with enough black treacle to smear thickly all over the bacon joint. Wrap up well in two or three layers of foil. Put into a roasting pan and cook in a low oven at Gas Mark 1/275°F/140°C for 3–4 hours, according to size.

Remove from the oven, unwrap, cut off the thick bacon skin while still hot and pour off any juices. Wrap again in foil, put heavy books or weights on top and leave to cool for 12 hours or overnight.

Then chill in the fridge and when you unwrap the foil sprinkle demerara sugar thickly all over the fat where the skin was taken off. As with most cold meats, this is most delicious if carved as thinly as possible.

HONEY PORK WITH RAISIN AND ROSEMARY STUFFING
Serves 6–8

Cold roast pork can be rather dry and dull. This way of stuffing it and cooking it in honey makes the joint particularly moist and full of flavour, while its glossy appearance is festive and inviting.

> 1–2 sprigs rosemary or 2 teaspoons
>   (2 × 5 ml spoon) dried rosemary
> 3–4 oz (75–100 g) seedless raisins
> 1–2 cloves garlic
> 2½-3½ lb (1–1.5 kg) rolled pork shoulder
>   or belly
> salt, black pepper
> approx. 2 tablespoons (2 × 15 ml spoon)
>   honey

Take the leaves off the rosemary sprigs and chop them up finely with the raisins and garlic. Press this mixture deep into the gaps in the meat or, if the meat hasn't been rolled yet by the butcher, spread the stuffing on, then roll up and tie securely with string. Sprinkle all over with salt and pepper. Then press the honey in with the raisin mixture and smear honey liberally all over the joint including the hard skin and fat, which should be scored first with a sharp knife. Put the meat on a piece of foil in a roasting pan. Bring the foil up round the joint, to keep the honey juices close around the meat, but leaving the hard skin on top exposed. Put on a high shelf in the oven at Gas Mark 7/425°F/220°C for 10 minutes until the top is turning golden brown. Then baste with the honey juices and bring the meat down on to a lower shelf. Turn down the oven to Gas Mark 3/325°F/160°C and cook, basting occasionally, for a further 2–2½ hours.

Put the meat on a plate to cool. Reserve the juices but pour off the excess fat. Put the juices in a pan and bubble fiercely for a minute or two until thickened. Brush this glaze all over the meat and then leave to become completely cold. Keep in the fridge and carve thinly.

HERRING AND APPLE IN SOURED CREAM
Serves 4

This delicious concoction only takes minutes to prepare, so eat it the same day when the apples are still crunchy. It is perfect as a first course or as a more interesting accompaniment to cold meat and salad.

2–3 (5–6 oz, 125–150 g) pickled herring fillets
1 carton fresh soured cream

1 medium size cooking apple – peeled and cut in small, thin pieces
1 small onion – sliced finely
½ teaspoon (2.5 ml spoon) grated or ground nutmeg
salt, black pepper
a little parsley to garnish

Rinse the fillets thoroughly under cold water, pat dry and cut them into small pieces. Mix in a bowl with the cream, apple, onion and nutmeg, adding salt and pepper to taste.

Transfer the mixture to a serving dish and sprinkle with chopped parsley. Serve with thin slices of brown bread.

COUNTRY VEAL TERRINE
Serves 18–20

This large terrine, turned out of its dish, neatly striped with bacon and glossy with its own delicious jelly, is a beautiful sight at a Christmas party, and although it is straightforward to do you are bound to feel triumphant! It can be made well in advance and kept in the fridge for up to two weeks. If you are unable to get veal you can use lean pork or even boned chicken instead.

For the marinade

1–1½ glasses sherry
1 heaped tablespoon (2 × 15 ml spoon)
*   soft brown sugar*
10 crushed allspice or juniper berries
approx. 8 peppercorns
1 heaped tablespoon (2 × 15 ml spoon)
*   finely chopped sage*
approx. 4 bay leaves
2–3 teaspoons (2–3 × 5 ml spoon) mixed
*   spice*
2 teaspoons (2 × 5 ml spoon) ground
*   mace or nutmeg*
plenty of salt and black pepper

For the terrine

1½ lb (600 g) pie veal
1 lb (400 g) belly of pork
¾ lb (300 g) pig's liver (minced through
*   the coarse blade of a mincer)*
¾ lb (300 g) thinly sliced smoked streaky
*   bacon*
4–5 black peppercorns or whole juniper
*   berries*

Mix the marinade ingredients together in a large dish. Mix the minced veal, belly of pork and pig's liver into the marinade mixture. Cover and leave for about 8 hours at room temperature.

Grease a 2-pt earthenware dish. Remove the bay leaves from the marinade and arrange on the bottom of the dish in a pattern with four or five peppercorns or juniper berries. Lay the bacon neatly in strips on the bottom and sides of the dish, reserving enough to lay on top of the terrine. Spoon the meat and marinade mixture into the dish. Lay the remaining strips of bacon on the top.

Cover with greased foil and then a lid and put the dish in a pan of water in the oven at Gas Mark 3/325°F/160°C for 1½-2 hours or until it starts to shrink away from the sides.

Cool for half an hour, then put a board and some weights or books on top of the dish (try to reserve any juice that spills over the sides) and leave for an hour or two.

Remove board and weights and chill in the fridge. The easiest way to turn the terrine on to a serving dish is to dip the dish in very hot water up to the rim for about half a minute or just until the terrine flops out when you turn it upside down and give it a good shake.

Melt any reserved jelly juices and brush the top of the terrine with them. Return to the fridge until you serve it.

RAVISHING ROULADE
Serves 5–6

This is a divine combination of pork fillet, turkey breast and ham, interspersed with a mixture of parsley, garlic, green peppercorns and anchovies, which impact a wonderful flavour to the rest. Despite its impressive appearance this savoury swiss roll is both fun and easy to make. It can be eaten hot, with perhaps potatoes and french beans, or it is delightful cold, sliced very thinly and arranged on a large serving plate with a salad.

12 oz (375 g) pork fillet
10–12 oz (300–375 g) turkey or chicken
*   breast fillets, skinned*
a large handful of chopped parsley
1–2 garlic cloves
1 rounded teaspoon (5 ml rounded
*   spoon) bottled green peppercorns*
2 oz (50 g) can of anchovy fillets
4 oz (125 g) sliced ham
lemon juice
olive oil
salt, black pepper

Lay the pork fillet on a sheet of greaseproof paper; slice into the meat lengthways to open it out, but don't cut right through. Lay another piece of greaseproof paper on

top and beat the meat out forcefully with a rolling pin so it becomes as thin as possible. Then, in the same way, beat out the turkey or chicken fillets. Chop the parsley, garlic, green peppercorns and anchovies finely and mix together, including the anchovy oil. Season to taste.

Spread a third of the parsley mixture on the flattened pork fillet. Cover with the turkey or chicken breasts and spread on more parsley; finally cover with the slices of ham and spread with the rest of the parsley mixture. Now roll up, starting from the short side, like a swiss roll. Carefully place the roll join-side down in a roasting pan and smear it all over with lemon juice and olive oil. Heat the oven to Gas Mark 2/300°F/150°C. Lay a piece of foil loosely over the meat and roast in the centre of the oven for 1¾–2 hours, basting occasionally and removing the foil about half-way through the cooking time. Move the meat carefully to a carving board, cut in fairly thin slices and lay these neatly in a serving dish.

FRUITED GALANTINE WITH PIGEON BREAST

Serves about 8

This galantine is simple to make and looks very pretty when cut in slices because the centre, encased within layers of bacon and chicken breast, is so unusual. It is a mixture of whole turkey livers and strips of pigeon breast, dotted with prunes and cashew nuts. The galatine is useful for any of those cold meals over Christmas, and a neat slice put on a plate, with a surround of salad leaves and a little cranberry sauce, makes a good first course.

1 wood pigeon
8 oz (250 g) turkey livers
2 oz (50 g) unsalted cashew nuts
2 oz (50 g) soft pitted prunes, chopped
    roughly
2 teaspoons (2 x 5ml spoon) chopped
    tarragon
3 large garlic cloves
2 skinned chicken breast fillets, weighing
    8–10 oz (250–300 g) in total
oil for greasing
10 oz (300 g) rindless smoked black
    bacon rashers
sea salt, black pepper

Using a sharp knife and keeping close to the bone, cut the breasts off the pigeon (keep the carcass for making stock). Skin the breast and cut them into thin strips. Put these into a bowl with the whole turkey livers. Mix in the cashew nuts and the chopped prunes and tarragon. Peel and slice the garlic and add to the mixture. Season with plenty of black pepper and a sprinkling of sea salt. Put the chicken breast fillets between two sheets of polythene or oiled greaseproof paper and bash them with a rolling pin until they are thin and spread out. Oil a 1 lb (500 g) loaf tin and line the sides and base with all but two or three of the bacon rashers. Then line the tin once more with the thin pieces of chicken breast, reserving some, with the bacon rashers, for the top. Now spoon the liver and pigeon mixture into the tin and top it up with the remaining pieces of chicken breast followed by the reserved rashers of bacon. Cover with foil. Put a roasting pan half-full of water in the centre of the oven and heat to Gas Mark 3/325°F/170°C. Put the tin in water for 2 hours.

Lift the foil, pour off the juices into a bowl and strain and reserve them in the fridge. Cover the galatine again with foil and then put a board on top and weigh it down with weights or books. Leave until cold. Dip the tin briefly in hot water and then shake out the galatine on to a board. To keep it in the fridge wrap it in cling film. Before serving, pu

he galatine on to a serving plate, melt the
uices and brush them over. Refrigerate until
eeded.

WHITE CABBAGE SALAD WITH BLUE CHEESE DRESSING

Serves 8
1 medium-size white cabbage (or
Chinese cabbage)
3–4 oz (75–100 g) piece of Danish blue
cheese
1 carton fresh soured cream
pinch of grated nutmeg
a little top of the milk or single cream

Slice the white cabbage finely and put in
a bowl. To make the dressing blend all
the other ingredients together (you can do
this in seconds with a liquidiser) adding
enough top of the milk to give a coating
consistency. Season to taste with salt and
black pepper.

RED CABBAGE, PARSNIP AND HAZELNUT SALAD

Serves 8

The subtle, sweet flavour of the parsnip is an
important part of this excellent winter salad.

For the salad
1 medium-size red cabbage
½ lb (200 g) small parsnips – boiled and
cut in quarters
2–3 oz (50–75 g) hazelnuts
1 dessertspoon (10 ml spoon) dried
fennel or tarragon
For the French dressing
3 tablespoons (3 × 15 ml spoon) red
wine vinegar
6 tablespoons (6 × 15 ml spoon) olive oil
1 teaspoon (5 ml spoon) soft brown
sugar
1 crushed clove garlic (optional)
salt, black pepper

Simply slice the red cabbage very finely and
mix in a bowl with the boiled parsnips and
hazelnuts. Sprinkle over the dried fennel. I find
the easiest way to mix the French dressing
is to have a jam jar with a tight-fitting lid kept
for the purpose so that you can vigorously
shake the ingredients up together.

PARSNIP SALAD WITH BRAZIL NUTS

Serves 6–8

You may think cooked parsnips would make an unlikely salad but in fact their subtle, slightly sweet flavour is most successful.

1 lb (400 g) small parsnips
3–4 sticks celery – sliced across rather finely
2 oz (50 g) shelled brazil nuts – chopped roughly
1 oz (25 g) candied peel
3 teaspoons (3 × 5 ml spoon) dried fennel or a handful of
parsley – finely chopped
French dressing with 2 teaspoons (2 × 5 ml spoon) French mustard added (see p.69)

Peel the parsnips and cut in quarters. Boil them in salted water (or better still, steam them) until just tender. Drain and cool. Then mix all the ingredients together in a salad bowl and dress. This is one of those salads which won't suffer if you dress it a little before you eat it.

WALNUT STUFFED BREAST OF VEAL

Serves 8–12

This deliciously stuffed joint can be prepared beforehand and will be ready to pop in your oven to provide yet another very special meal over Christmas. Alternatively, you can eat the joint cold or use the stuffing recipe as one of the stuffings for the turkey.

2½-3 lb (1–1.4 kg) boned breast of veal
2 oz (50 g) fresh breadcrumbs
good handful of parsley – chopped finely
3–4 oz (75–100 g) walnuts – chopped small
1 teaspoon (5 ml spoon) dried thyme or oregano
2 cloves garlic – crushed
salt, black pepper
1 lightly whisked egg
oil

If the veal has already been rolled up and tied cut the string and lay the meat flat. Into a mixing bowl put the breadcrumbs, chopped parsley, walnuts, thyme, garlic, salt and plenty of black pepper. Mix together and then mix in the egg. Spread this mixture and press down over the meat. Then roll up and tie together with string. Smear the joint all over with oil and rub a little salt on the fat on the top. Roast in the centre of the oven at Gas Mark 3/325°F/160°C for 2–2½ hours, basting occasionally.

BEAN SALAD WITH LEMON AND MUSTARD DRESSING
Serves 8

Dried beans are so useful for winter salads. It is said that they cook better if you soak them in rainwater: I have tried this but can't say that I can notice a difference!

For the salad
½ lb (200 g) dried haricot or red kidney
    beans
¾ lb (300 g) frozen French beans
1 large onion – chopped finely
1 red pepper – sliced thinly (optional)
For the dressing
juice of 1 lemon
4–5 tablespoons (4–5 × 15 ml spoon)
    olive oil
1 teaspoon (5 ml spoon) honey
2 teaspoons (2 × 5 ml spoon) mild
    French mustard
salt, black pepper

Soak the dried beans in cold water overnight. Boil in unsalted water until tender – about ½-1 hour, but the cooking time depends on the age of the beans. Rinse with cold water and drain. Cook the French beans in boiling, salted water for 2–3 minutes – they should still be slightly crunchy. Drain and mix in a salad bowl with the haricot beans, chopped onion and red pepper. Put the dressing ingredients into an empty jam jar with a lid and shake thoroughly. Pour over the salad and toss.

EGG, MUSHROOM AND PIMENTO SALAD
Serves 6

A satisfying salad which can also be used as a first course to a meal.

1 carton fresh soured cream
2 heaped tablespoons (4 × 15 ml spoon)
    mayonnaise
3–4 teaspoons (3–4 × 5 ml spoon) mild
    French mustard
½ level teaspoon (2.5 ml spoon) ground
    cinnamon
black pepper, salt
4 sliced hardboiled eggs
1 large green or red pimento – sliced very
    thinly
½ lb (200 g) mushrooms – sliced thinly
chopped parsley for garnish

In a large bowl mix together the cream and the mayonnaise until smooth. Add the mustard, cinnamon, salt and black pepper to taste. Stir in the prepared pimento and mushrooms and lastly the sliced eggs. Transfer the mixture to a serving bowl and decorate the edges with chopped parsley.

OLD-FASHIONED SPICED BEEF
Serves 6–8

A good piece of spiced beef is particularly appropriate at Christmas time. It has a subtle, mellow flavour and can be carved in paper-thin slices. Either buy prepared salt meat or salt your own, using a method to be found in any standard recipe book.

3–4 lb (1.25–1.5 kg) joint of boned, salt
    silverside or brisket
black pepper
soft dark brown sugar (Muscovado or
    Barbados)
1 level tablespoon (15 ml spoon) whole
    allspice berries
1 level tablespoon (15 ml spoon) juniper
    berries
approx. 1 dessertspoon (10 ml spoon)
    cloves

First soak the joint in cold water for 2–4 hours, changing the water once or twice. Sprinkle the joint generously with black pepper. Rub the brown sugar quite thickly all over the joint. Crush the allspice and juniper berries in a mortar, liquidiser or coffee grinder and press all over the joint and into any cracks. I usually make one or two incisions to get some spices right to the centre of the meat.

Stick the cloves into the joint all over. Wrap the joint up very thoroughly in foil and place in a large ovenproof dish with a well fitting lid, or in a roasting pan with more foil on top. If possible leave like this at room temperature overnight.

Cook in the centre of the oven Gas Mark 1/275°F/140°C for about 3½-4½ hours, according to the size of the joint. Take out, open the foil slightly to let the juices pour away and wrap the foil round the joint again. Then leave in a cool place with a board and books or weights on top until the next day.

Keep it in the fridge in foil until you want to carve it. Carve as thinly as possible. Wrap up any leftover piece in foil again and store in the fridge. If you have had cranberry sauce with your turkey, this goes very well with the beef.

POTATO AND MUSHROOM SALAD
Serves 6

This is another more substantial salad which goes especially well with cold meat.

For the salad
1 lb (400 g) small potatoes
8 oz (200 g) button mushrooms
large bunch parsley – finely chopped

For the dressing
2 tablespoons (2 × 15 ml spoon) mayonnaise – a good bought kind will do
3 tablespoons (3 × 15 ml spoon) plain yoghurt
1–2 teaspoons (1–2 × 5 ml spoon) mild French mustard
salt, black pepper

Scrape (don't peel) the potatoes and boil until done. Cool and then slice. Slice the mushrooms downwards, keeping the stalk on so that they are a flat mushroom shape. Put all into a bowl with the chopped parsley.

To make the dressing simply stir up the ingredients with a fork until smooth, adding a little salt and plenty of black pepper. Coat the salad ingredients with this mixture and keep in the fridge until needed.

TOMATO AND SAGE SALAD
Serves 4–6

During the summer tomato salads are incomparably improved by the addition of fresh basil, and chopped fresh mint is very good too. In mid-winter it is difficult to find fresh herbs, other than greenhouse parsley, but the sage bush struggles on without losing all its leaves.

1–1½ lb (400–600 g) sliced tomatoes
good handful fresh sage leaves
French dressing (see p. 69)

Get a good handful of leaves and chop them very finely before adding to a tomato salad. Dress with a French dressing just before serving.

CELERY, RED CABBAGE AND SPRING ONION SALAD

Serves 8

If you can find them, fennel roots are even better than celery in this salad, but celery is specially good at this time of year.

1 bunch celery
1 small red cabbage
1–2 bunches spring onions
yoghurt and mustard dressing (see
    p. 73)

Slice the celery across in thinnish pieces and thinly slice the red cabbage. Take the outer leaves and the roots off the spring onions and slice in small pieces using as much of the green stem as possible. Mix all together and dress with the yoghurt and mustard dressing made to the recipe given in Potato and Mushroom Salad.

CUCUMBER, OLIVE AND WALNUT SALAD

Serves 6–8

Here is my adaptation of an old English recipe for an unusual and decorative cucumber salad. I find that the cream dressing instead of mayonnaise goes particularly well.

For the salad
1 medium sized cucumber
4 oz (100 g) stoned green olives –
    chopped
3 oz (75 g) shelled walnuts – chopped
juice of ½ lemon
a few large lettuce leaves
For the dressing
1 carton fresh soured cream
3 tablespoons (3 × 15 ml spoon) single
    cream
2 teaspoons (2 × 5 ml spoon) dried
    tarragon or chives
salt, black pepper

Peel the cucumber and chop up into cubes. Mix it in a bowl with the chopped chives, the walnuts and the lemon juice. Arrange the leutuce leaves on a serving dish and then spoon the cucumber mixture on top. Mix the dressing ingredients together until smooth and pour over the salad.

BOXING DAY SAUCE
Serves 6–8

A quickly made curried sauce with a beautiful sheen to it and a refreshing flavour which will revive even the driest cold turkey.

> *5 fl oz (125 ml) mayonnaise (a good*
> *bought kind will do)*
> *10 fl oz (250 ml) plain yoghurt*
> *a little orange juice (to taste)*
> *1–3 teaspoons (1–3 × 5 ml spoon) curry*
> *powder*
> *a little tomato purée (optional)*
> *salt*

Mix the mayonnaise and yoghurt smoothly together. Stir in the orange juice, curry powder, tomato purée and salt to taste. Either spread the sauce over a dish of carved, cold turkey or put out in a bowl for people to spoon on to their plates.

MINCE PIES AND DESSERTS

I don't think there's any comparison between homemade and shop-bought mince pies. The mincemeat can be made months ahead and looks most satisfying as it matures on the larder shelf, while the rich pastry is even more melting if you can make it in advance and keep it in your freezer. However, some people, especially children, don't really like Christmas pudding, or even mince pies, so it is good to have something sweet and refreshing but still seasonal as an alternative.

MINCE PIES DE LUXE
For 24 mince pies

Mince pies can be rather dry but here the mixture of the spicy mincemeat with smooth cream cheese makes them a real luxury.

8 oz (200 g) full cream cheese
2 oz (50 g) caster sugar
1 lb (400 g) orange pastry (see recipe on p.77)
1–1¼ lb (400–500 g) mincemeat
a spot of milk
caster or icing sugar for dusting

First put the cream cheese and the 2 oz caster sugar into a bowl and beat until smooth. Knead the pastry lightly and roll out rather more thickly than usual. Using a 3 in. (7 cm) fluted pastry cutter, cut out 24 rounds, re-rolling the pastry as necessary, and line greased patty tins with the rounds. Fill to about half their depth with mincemeat.

Then put a teaspoonful of the beaten cream cheese mixture on top of the mincemeat and smooth over. Roll out the remaining pastry and with a smaller fluted cutter, 2¼ in. (5 cm), cut out another 24 rounds. Moisten the underside of the rounds and place them on top of the filled pies. Press the edges lightly together and make a small slit in the top of each pie. Brush with cold milk and bake in the centre of the oven, preheated to Gas Mark 7/425°F/220°C for 15–20 minutes until light golden brown. The pastry is so deliciously crumbly that it is best to let these mince pies cool down before gently easing them from the tins with a round-bladed knife.

Before serving either warm – which of course is best – or cold, sprinkle them generously with caster or icing sugar.

ORANGE PASTRY FOR MINCE PIES
For 24 mince pies

This light, crumbly, rich pastry really compliments home-made mincemeat. To try and alleviate any last-minute panic, I always make a large batch of mince pies beforehand and put them in the freezer. I take them out and heat them up as I need them and they taste perfect.

1 lb (400 g) plain flour
8 oz (200 g) butter
4 oz (100 g) lard
grated rind of 1 large orange
orange juice

Cut the fat into the flour and rub with your fingertips until it resembles breadcrumbs. Stir in the grated rind.

With a knife, stir the orange juice into the pastry until it just begins to stick together (if there isn't enough juice add a spot of cold water). Gather into a ball, wrap in foil or plastic and put into the fridge for half an hour or more before using.

TRADITIONAL MINCEMEAT
Makes 9–10 lb (3.5–4.0 kg)

Originally, lean beef was the important ingredient which earned this indispensable Christmas pie filling its name. I wonder why it was dropped from the recipe over the years (the first edition of Mrs Beeton is the last time we hear of it), as the beef seems to give a lovely mild taste.

It makes a costlier mixture but the best I have tasted and I feel it is a tradition worth reviving. This quantity makes 9–10 lb of mincemeat, so halve the quantity if you like, though it keeps well and I find it useful for school fairs or little presents.

1 lb (400 g) seedless raisins
1½ lb (600 g) currants
¾ lb (300 g) lean rump steak – with any
*   fat trimmed off and then minced*
1½ lb (600 g) shredded beef suet
1 lb (400 g) soft dark brown sugar
4 oz (100 g) chopped mixed peel
½ whole nutmeg – freshly grated

2 lbs (800 g) cooking apples – peeled,
   cored and either chopped finely or
   minced
grated rind and juice of 1 lemon
¼ pt (125 ml) (or a little more) brandy

Thoroughly mix all the ingredients together in the order given. Stir in the lemon juice and brandy. Press closely into jars to exclude air. Leave for at least a fortnight before using.

APRICOT AND PINEAPPLE MINCEMEAT

Makes 6–8 jars

It is always worth making more jars of mincemeat than you need, because a pretty jar will make a perfect contribution to a Christmas bazaar or a present for a friend. I like a tang to my mincemeat and here apricots give exactly the right sharpness.

1 lb (500 g) dried apricots, chopped finely
12 oz (375 g) crystallized pineapple,
   chopped finely
4 oz (125 g) glace cherries, chopped
12 oz (375 g) currants
12 oz (375 g) candied peel, chopped
   finely
12 oz (375 g) dessert apples, peeled,
   cored and chopped finely

4 oz (125 g) blanched almonds, chopped
1 lb (500 g) soft dark brown sugar
6 oz (175 g) shredded suet
1 level teaspoon (5 ml level spoon)
   ground cloves
2 teaspoons (2 x 5 ml spoon) ground
   cinnamon
coarsely grated rind and juice of 2 lemons
coarsely grated rind and juice of 1 large
   orange
½ pint (300 ml) brandy

Put the prepared dried fruit, peel, apples and almonds in a large mixing bowl. Stir in the sugar, suet and spices. Then add the lemon and orange rind and juice and the brandy and mix together well. Cover the bowl and leave in a cool place for two days.

Stir again, adding a little more brandy if the mixture seems at all dry and pack into clean, dry jars. Cover the jars and leave in a cool place for two weeks or more before using.

DATE AND WALNUT MINCEMEAT
Makes approx. 8 lb (3 kg)

This is a good, spicy variation of the normal mincemeat mixture. It should keep well for two or three years, but if it seems to dry out add a little more rum or brandy.

8 oz (200 g) stoned dates
8 oz (200 g) raisins
8 oz (200 g) sultanas
4 oz (100 g) dried apricots or glacé
  cherries
8 oz (200 g) cooking apples – peeled
  and cored
6 oz (150 g) walnuts
4 oz (100 g) mixed peel
8 oz (200 g) shredded suet
10 oz (250 g) demerara sugar
1 level teaspoon (5 ml spoon) ground
  cinnamon
1 level teaspoon (5 ml spoon) ground
  nutmeg
1 level teaspoon (5 ml spoon) ground
  cloves
grated rind and juice of 2 large lemons
3–6 fl oz (75–150 ml) dark rum or brandy

Finely chop or mince the prepared fruit, peel, apples and nuts. Add the suet, sugar and spices and the grated lemon rind and juice. Stir in enough rum or brandy to give a moist mixture. Cover and leave for two days. Stir thoroughly again, put into clean jars and store in a cool place.

CELEBRATION ICE CREAM
Serves 6–8

This luxurious winter ice cream made with dried fruit, nuts and port is a real treat to look forward to at Christmas. It has a beautifully rich, smooth texture and has the advantage of not having to be stirred or whisked half-way through the freezing. It is bound to make a most popular finale to one of your family feasts ! If your family really don't like Christmas pudding this can be an exciting alternative.

6 oz (150 g) currants
¼ pt (125 ml) port
4 large (size 2) eggs
¼ teaspoon (½ × 2.5 ml spoon) salt
8 oz (200 g) sugar
¼ pt (125 ml) water
4 oz (100 g) shelled walnuts – roughly
  chopped
2 oz (50 g) chopped candied peel
2 oz (50 g) glacé cherries – roughly
  chopped
½ pt (250 ml) double or whipping cream
a few nuts and halved glacé cherries and
  angelica for decoration (optional)

Put the currants and port into a saucepan and heat to simmering. Remove from heat and leave until the port is cool. Put the eggs and salt into a mixing bowl and whisk until frothy. Put the sugar and water into a small saucepan.

Bring to the boil and boil fiercely for 3 minutes. Immediately, pour this syrup in a thin stream on the frothy eggs while whisking all the time at high speed (an electric whisk is easiest for this but if you have only a hand one try to get someone else to pour the sugar syrup in, while you whisk). To help the mixture cool quickly, put the hot bowl in a sink of cold water and stir. Whip the cream until thick but not stiff. Stir the currants, port, nuts, peel and cherries into the cooled egg mixture and lastly fold in the whipped cream. Transfer to a serving bowl and freeze.

When frozen decorate, if you like, with cherries, nuts and cut-out leaves of angelica.

DRIED FRUIT COMPOTE WITH GINGER AND RUM
Serves 4–6

An excellent winter fruit salad with the most aromatic juices, which makes a refreshing dessert at Christmas time. It will keep well in the fridge.

> *2 × 8 oz (2 × 200 g) packets dried mixed fruit (apricots, apples, etc. – cut any extra-large fruits in half)*
> *2 oz (50 g) crystallised ginger – cut into small pieces*
> *2–4 oz (50–100 g) demerara or granulated sugar*
> *juice of 2 lemons and 1 orange*
> *2–3 tablespoons (2–3 × 15 ml spoon) dark rum*

Soak the dried fruit overnight or for at least 6 hours. Drain it and put into a large saucepan with the ginger, sugar and fruit juice. Bring to the boil, then cover and simmer gently for half an hour. Then stir in the rum, transfer to a serving bowl and let cool. Serve with cream.

SNOWBALL PUDDING
Serves 6–8

I love this chilled pudding because its easy to make, looks like a snow-white Christmas pudding and tastes very good indeed. You could have it, decorated with holly, as an alternative to Christmas pudding or as a dessert at another meal. Unlike Christmas pudding, there's no question that the children might not like it – I find it universally popular.

8 oz (200 g) full cream cheese
3 oz (75 g) caster sugar
3 oz (75 g) melted unsalted butter
2 oz (50 g) chopped hazelnuts
1 oz (25 g) candied peel
2 oz (50 g) chopped glacé cherries
2 oz (50 g) chopped crystallised ginger
grated rind and juice of 2 oranges and 1 lemon
8 trifle sponges
½ oz (2 × 5 ml spoon) or 1 packet gelatine
¼ pt (125 ml) double or whipping cream

Beat the cream cheese with the sugar and the melted butter until smooth and creamy. Stir in the chopped nuts, candied peel, chopped ginger and cherries and the grated rind of the oranges and lemon. Slice the sponges crossways into 3 thin slices each.

Put 3 or 4 slices on the bottom of a 2-pt pudding basin. Then spoon a layer of the cream cheese mixture, then another layer of sponges, and so on, ending with a layer of sponges. Dilute the juice of the oranges and lemon to ¾ pt (375 ml), with hot water.

Dissolve the gelatine in a cup with 2 tablespoons of very hot water and stir it into the juices. Strain the juice over the mixture in the pudding basin, making sure the juice gets to the bottom of the basin by pulling the mixture back with a spoon.

Put in the fridge to set. When well chilled, dip the basin briefly in hot water and turn out on to a serving plate. Whisk the cream until thick and ice the pudding with it. Decorate the top with a sprig of holly. Chill again in the fridge before serving.

CRANBERRY CASKET FILLED WITH GOLD
Serves 8

Here is a truly spectacular finale to a festive meal. The pudding looks like a fantasy; a bright scarlet, crumpled flower with ragged petals, holding in its open bud something creamy, yellow and tempting. The scarlet case is, in fact, a cranberry sorbet and it is filled with a mango, lemon and rum ice cream. You can make this well ahead and eat it straight from the freezer.

9 oz (275 g) fresh cranberries
5 oz (150 g) granulated sugar
juice of 2 oranges
2 large egg whites (size 1–2)
8 oz (250 g) demerara sugar
¼ pint (150 ml) lemon juice
½ pint (300 ml) whipping cream
2 ripe mangoes
3–4 tablespoons (3–4 x 15 ml spoons) rum

Put the cranberries into a saucepan with the granulated sugar and the orange juice. Bring to the boil, stirring to dissolve the sugar, and then cover and simmer for about 8 minutes until the cranberries are mushy. Now whizz this cranberry mixture to a purée in a food processor and leave it to cool.

When the purée is cold line a deep bowl (at least 3-pint (1.75-litre) capacity) with non-stick baking parchment, folding it so that it fits the shape of the bowl. The edges of the paper should come above the edge of the bowl; they will be uneven but this doesn't matter. Spoon the cooled cranberry purée into the paper-lined bowl and, using a wide knife or spatula, smear it up the sides of the bowl, leaving an uneven edge. Put the bowl in the freezer for an hour or more. If you have too much mixture for your bowl, it's nice to make a second, smaller casket in a smaller bowl, which you can put in the centre of the large one.

Make the mango ice cream. Whisk the egg whites until they stand in soft peaks. Put the demerara sugar into a deepish pouring saucepan with the lemon juice. Dissolve the sugar with the lemon juice, stirring over a low heat. When the sugar has dissolved bring it to the boil and let it bubble fiercely, without stirring, for 3 minutes. Pour the bubbling liquid in a thin stream on to the egg whites, whisking all the time at high speed. Continue whisking until the mixture is thick.

In another bowl, whisk the cream until thick but not too stiff. Fold the cream into the mixture with a metal spoon. Cut the mangoes in half (do this on a board in the sink as it can be messy) and cut and scrape as much flesh as you can off the stone and skin. Put the flesh in a food processor with the rum and whizz it to purée. Fold the purée gently but thoroughly into the cream and egg-white mixture. Take the cranberry bowl from the freezer, pour the mango mixture into it and then freeze again overnight.

Lift the frozen casket out of the metal bowl with the edge of the paper. Gently peel off all the paper and put your casket on a serving plate. Put it back in the freezer until you are ready to serve it.

ORANGE AND ALMOND TART
Serves 8

Here is something lovely to serve either instead of mince pies or simply as a pudding. Like mince pies, it goes beautifully with brandy butter. As with mince pies also the tart can be made well in advance, frozen and then re-heated before serving.

For the pastry
8 oz (250g) plain flour
3 tablespoons (3 x 15 ml spoons) caster sugar
5 oz (150 g) butter, plus extra for greasing
1 tablespoon (15 ml spoon) water
For the filling
1 medium-size, thin-skinned orange
½ small thin-skinned lemon
4 tablespoons (4 x 15 ml spoons) double cream
1 large egg (size 1–2)
3 oz (75 g) caster sugar
½ teaspoon (2.5 ml spoon) ground cloves
2 oz (50 g) ground almonds
2–3 oz (50–75 g) whole blanched almonds
icing sugar

Lightly butter a 9½-inch (24 cm), loose-based, aluminium, fluted flan tin. To make the pasty, sift the flour in a bowl. Stir in the caster sugar. Gently melt the butter with the water in a saucepan. Then pour slowly into the flour mixing it in thoroughly with a wooden spoon to form a dough. Now take up pieces of the warm dough and press it as evenly as possible over the base and up the sides of the flan tin. Refrigerate while you prepare the flan filling.

Cut the oranges into quarters and pick out any pips. Cut the half lemon in half and again extract any pips. Put the orange and lemon pieces into a food processor with the cream, the egg, the caster sugar and the ground cloves. Whizz through thoroughly to a mush. Then briefly whizz in the ground almonds. Heat the oven to Gas Mark 4/350°F/180°C. Spread the fairly thick filling mixture evenly into the chilled pastry case. Carefully lay lines of blanched almonds fanning out from the centre of the tart in a fairly close 'starburst' pattern. Bake in the centre of the oven for 35–40 minutes until browned and evenly risen, turning the tart round once or twice so that the pastry edges brown evenly.

Leave the tart in the tin for 8–10 minutes; then push it out and slide it carefully off the base of the tin on to a serving plate. Serve warm with cream or brandy butter. Sift some icing sugar over the top for a festive appearance.

PINEAPPLE CHOCOLATE CRUNCH GÂTEAU
Serves 10

This is a rich and sumptuous pudding suitable for any Christmas Party. Fresh pineapple is crystallized and then, with other glace fruits and nuts, tops two crunchy layers of dark chocolate sandwiched together with a light cheesecake cream. It is delectable.

1 large pineapple
oil for greasing
10 oz (300 g) plain chocolate
2 oz (50 g) unsalted butter
1 tablespoon (15 ml spoon) hot water
4 sponge fingers
4 oz (125 g) candied peel
4 oz (125 g) glacé cherries, chopped
juice of 1 lemon
12 oz (375 g) granulated sugar
½ pint (300 ml) double cream
2 oz (50 g) icing sugar, sifted
2 oz (50 g) curd cheese
2 tablespoons (2 x 15 ml spoons) natural yogurt

To decorate
glacé cherries
angelica
1 tablespoon (15 ml spoon) flaked almonds

Cut the pineapple into slices approximately ½-inch (1 cm) thick or less. Cut off the skin, using a sharp knife, and remove the core with an apple corer. Put the pineapple rings in the bottom of a large, heavy saucepan and just cover them with water. Cover the pan, bring to the boil and simmer for ¾–1 hour until the fruit is soft when you push a knife through it.

Meanwhile, oil the sides of two 8–8 ½-inch (20–21 cm) sandwich tins and put a disc of greaseproof paper on the bottom of each. Melt the chocolate in a bowl over a pan half-full of barely simmering water. Add the butter and hot water. Break up the sponge fingers roughly and stir them into the chocolate, together with the candied peel and chopped glace cherries. Spread this mixture over the bottoms on the tins and leave it to set in the fridge.

When the pineapple is ready, remove the slices from the pan with a slotted spoon and put them on one side. Boil the water in the pan fiercely until it has reduced to about ½ pint (300 ml) – keep watch as this won't take long – and then add the lemon juice and granulated sugar. Dissolve the sugar over a low heat, add the pineapple rings and boil, uncovered, over a high heat for 8–20 minutes, skimming at first, until the pineapple

looks golden and translucent and the syrup has reduced and thickened; don't leave it too long, or it will become toffee-like. Transfer the rings to a piece of greaseproof paper to cool and reserve the syrup in the pan.

When the pineapple is quite cold, loosen the edges of one chocolate disc with a knife, turn it out and peel off the greaseproof paper. Put the disc smooth-side down, on a serving plate. Whisk the cream until it is softly thick, stir in the icing sugar and then whisk in the curd cheese and yogurt until the mixture is smooth and thick. Spread this on to the disc of chocolate. Place the second disc, rough-side down, on top of the cream. Arrange the pineapple rings in an overlapping pattern over the top. Cut some glacé cherries in half and arrange them over the holes in the rings. Cut a strip of angelica into leaf shapes or diamonds and arrange the decoratively round the cherries. Stir the flaked almonds in a frying pan over a high heat for a minute or two until browned and then scatter them over the top. Shortly before serving, spoon the reserved pineapple syrup on top of the gâteau.

ICED CHOCOLATE CHARLOTTE
Serves 10-12

Some puddings make people groan with pleasure: this is one of them. It's a luxurious ice cream, intensely chocolaty, within a case of sponge fingers soaked in a fresh orange and brandy syrup. Definitely and extravagant treat and perfect for the Christmas festivities. You can make it days ahead and it is enough for a large number of people.

½ pint (300 ml) unsweetened fresh
orange juice
juice of 1 lemon
6 oz (175 g) demerara sugar
2 tablespoons (2 x 15 ml spoons) brandy
25 sponge fingers
7 oz (200 g) plain chocolate
1 rounded tablespoon (15 ml rounded
spoon) cocoa powder
warm water
2 teaspoons (2 x 5 ml spoons) vanilla
essence
6 oz (175 g) soft dark brown sugar
2 large eggs (size 1–2)
a pinch of salt
1 pint (600 ml) whipping cream
4 rounded tablespoons (4 x 15 ml
rounded spoons) natural yogurt

Put the oranges and lemon juice in a largish saucepan, with the demerara sugar. Heat gently, stirring until the sugar has dissolved, and then bring to the boil and boil vigorously for 3–4 minutes until syrupy. Remove from the heat and stir in the brandy. Lay the sponge fingers in a roasting pan or shallow dish, unsugared-side downwards, and spoon the syrup over them. Leave for an hour or two, occasionally spooning any syrup which seeps out over them again.

Melt 5 oz (150 g) of chocolate in a bowl over hot but not boiling water, remove from the heat and put on one side. Put the cocoa powder in a mixing jug with 2 tablespoons of warm water and stir until smooth. Gradually add more water until you have 6 fl oz (175 ml). Add the vanilla essence. Pour into a largish saucepan and add the soft brown sugar. Break the eggs into a bowl of an electric mixer with a pinch of salt and whisk until they are frothy and thickened. Put the sugar and cocoa mixture over a gentle heat and stir until the sugar has dissolved. Then bring it to the boil and boil briskly for 3 minutes. Pour it in a thin stream on to the eggs, whisking all the time a high speed. Continue whisking for 2–3 minutes. Lastly, whisk in the melted chocolate thoroughly.

Now arrange the syrup-soaked sponge fingers closely together round the sides of an 8-inch (20 cm) deep cake tin with the unsugared side of the fingers against the tin. Spoon any remaining syrup on to the bottom of the tin. Whisk the cream until thick but not too stiff. Fold in the yogurt and gently fold this into the chocolate and egg mixture. Coarsely grate or chop up the remaining 2 oz (50 g) chocolate and stir it in to the mixture. Spoon slowly into the sponge-lined tin on top of the syrup. Freeze for several hours.

To unmould, dip the tin briefly in a sink of very hot water until you can turn it upside-down, and shake the chocolate charlotte out on to a serving plate. Put it back in the freezer, but take it out about an hour before eating and leave it in a cool place so that it reaches the best consistency.

CRANBERRY AND CHOCOLATE SURPRISE BOMBE

Serves 6–8

This combination of cranberries and dark chocolate with a centre of lemon syllabub is quite simply scrumptious. Because of the syllabub it is a pudding which shouldn't be made more than a day in advance but it is not time-consuming to prepare and really is an exciting treat with which to end a festive meal.

9 oz (275 g) fresh cranberries
5 oz (150 g) caster sugar
5 tablespoons (5 x 15 ml spoons) water
2 tablespoons (2 x 15 ml spoons) dark rum
1 lemon
5 oz (150 g) plain chocolate
½ pint (300 ml) double cream
2 oz (50 g) icing sugar, sifted

Put all but three or four of the cranberries into a saucepan with the caster sugar and 3 tablespoons of water. Stir over a medium heat until the sugar has dissolved. Then cover the pan and let it simmer for 6–8 minutes until all of the berries have popped and the consistency is mushy and very thick. Remove from the heat and stir in the rum. Leave the mixture to become completely cold. Then spoon it into a 2-pint (1.2-litre) pudding basin and spread it up the sides to line it thickly and as evenly as possible.

Finely grate the lemon rind and squeeze out the juice of half the lemon. Whisk the cream until it is beginning to thicken. Then whisk in the sifted icing sugar and continue whisking until the cream holds soft peaks: it should not be too stiff. Very gradually stir in the lemon juice with a metal spoon; then stir in the grated rind. Spoon this syllabub into the centre of the cranberry-lined basin and refrigerate for at least 6 hours.

Break the chocolate up into small pieces and put it with 2 tablespoons of water in a bowl set over a saucepan of very hot, but not boiling, water. Stir now and then until melted and smooth. Then remove from the heat and allow to cool for 10–15 minutes. Take the cranberry basin out of the fridge, dip it into a sink of very hot water for a minute or two and then turn it out, giving a firm shake, on to a serving plate. Slowly spoon the melted chocolate over the mound of cranberries as evenly as you can. Top the mound with the reserved cranberries and refrigerate it again until you are ready to eat.

ORANGE CHOCOLATE TRUFFLES

Makes about 20

Soft, fresh truffles, made at home with fresh cream and butter, must be the most luxurious and pleasurable of sweets. They are the finishing touch at any special occasion and would make an ideal Christmas present, too. A delicious variation on the orange flavour is to add peppermint essence to the mixture instead of orange rind.

> *8 oz (250 g) plain chocolate*
> *3 oz (75 g) unsalted butter, at room*
> *   temperature*
> *2 tablespoons (2 x 15 ml spoons) double*
> *   cream*
> *2 oz (50g) ground almonds*
> *finely grated rind of 1 orange*
> *1 tablespoon (15 ml spoon) drinking*
> *   chocolate powder*
> *1 teaspoon (5 ml spoon) cinnamon*

Break up the chocolate and put it in a bowl set over a pan half-full of very hot water, over a gentle heat; the water should not boil. Melt the chocolate and then add the butter, a little at a time, and then stir in the cream. Stir until melted and smooth and then remove from the heat and stir in the ground almonds and grated orange rind.

Let the mixture cool and then put it in the fridge until stiff enough to mould into balls. To do this, take up bits of the chocolate mixture with wet hands and lightly pat them into balls about the size of marbles. Put them on a sheet of greaseproof paper laid on a flat tin or board and return to the fridge until firm. Then mix the chocolate powder and cinnamon together and roll the truffles in this mixture to coat them thoroughly. If possible keep the truffles in the fridge or cool place until needed.

SEASONAL CAKES

However much food you have over Christmas the decorated cake, like the Christmas tree, is something you can't really do without. However, as long as its decorated appearance evokes Christmas cheer, it doesn't have to be a solid traditional cake covered with thick marzipan and rock-hard icing. Here are some mouthwatering alternatives.

YULE LOG
Serves 6–8

You may prefer, like the French, to have a rich chocolate log at Christmas instead of Christmas cake (or have it as well). This one, made with ground hazelnuts instead of flour, is light and luscious.

5 large (size 4) eggs – separated
5 oz (125 g) caster sugar
3 oz (75 g) ground hazelnuts (whizz up the whole nuts for a moment in either a liquidiser or coffee grinder) or ground almonds
1½ level teaspoons (3 × 2.5 ml spoon) baking powder
2 rounded tablespoons (3 × 15 ml spoon) cocoa powder, finely sifted
2–3 tablespoons (2–3 × 15 ml spoon) warm water

¼ teaspoon (½ × 2.5 ml spoon) cream of tartar
icing sugar
apricot jam
½ pt (250 ml) double cream

Heat the oven to Gas Mark 4/350°F/180°C. Lightly oil a large swiss roll tin measuring approximately 14 in. × 10 in. (35 cm × 25 cm). Line the bottom with a piece of greaseproof paper, also lightly oiled. Whisk the yolks of the eggs with the sugar until pale and fairly thick, but not stiff. Stir in the hazelnuts, baking powder and the cocoa powder and add the water to soften the mixture. Add the cream of tartar to the egg whites and whisk until stiff. Using a metal spoon, fold them gently but thoroughly into the yolk mixture.

90

Pour into the prepared tin and bake in the centre of the oven for about 20–25 minutes until springy to touch in the centre. Remove the tin from the oven, and leave to cool. The cake will now shrink a little, but that's normal. When cool, cover with greaseproof paper and a cloth and leave in the fridge for 2–3 hours, or overnight if possible. Then loosen the edges carefully with a knife.

Sprinkle a piece of greaseproof paper generously with sieved icing sugar. Turn the cake out on to the icing sugar and remove the oiled paper. Spread with apricot jam. Whip the cream until thick and spread on top of the jam.

Roll up with the help of the greaseproof paper, carefully and rather loosely. It will probably crack a bit but the cracks make it look like a real snow-covered log. Transfer to a serving dish. Sprinkle more icing sugar all over through a sieve and decorate with red-berried holly.

GLOSSY FRUIT AND WALNUT CHRISTMAS CAKE
Serves 6–8

If, like my family, you can easily do without marzipan and the hard icing covering of the Christmas cake, and find the cake itself rather too similar to the Christmas pudding, here is an alternative which is much less trouble and can look equally festive. It is a dark, moist cake, packed with fruit and nuts. Make it several weeks in advance if possible.

For the cake
8 oz (200 g) raisins
4 oz (100 g) currants
4 oz (100 g) sultanas
6 oz (150 g) dried apricots – chopped
    into small pieces
2 oz (50 g) mixed peel
3–4 tablespoons (3–4 × 15 ml spoon)
    rum or brandy
8 oz (200 g) self-raising flour
good pinch of salt
½ whole nutmeg – grated
6 oz (150 g) soft dark brown sugar
6 oz (150 g) butter
8 oz (200 g) chopped walnuts
2 large (size 4) beaten eggs
1 tablespoon (15 ml spoon) black treacle
    dissolved in a tablespoon of warm milk

For the glaze and decoration
angelica
glacé cherries
¾ lb (300 g) redcurrant jelly
preserving sugar or coffee sugar crystals
silver balls (optional)

The night before you make the cake put the fruit with the rum or brandy in a bowl, stir well together, put a cloth on top and leave overnight. The next day, heat the oven to Gas Mark 4/350°F/180°C. Grease and line a 8–9 in. (20–22 cm) round cake tin with greased greaseproof paper.

Put the flour, salt, nutmeg and sugar into a mixing bowl. Cut the butter into small lumps and rub it well into the flour and sugar with your fingers. Stir in the fruit, alcohol, and the chopped walnuts. Thoroughly stir in the beaten eggs and then the treacle dissolved in milk.

Put the mixture into the cake tin and bake in the centre of the oven. After half an hour turn the oven down to Gas Mark 2/300°F/150°C for about another 1¼-1¾ if hours until a sharp knife stuck into the centre comes out clean. If the cake looks as if it is getting too brown place a sheet of foil or brown paper on the top. Remove from the oven and leave in the tin for about 5 minutes, then loosen the edges carefully with a knife and turn out the right way up on a cooling tray. When cool, wrap in two layers of greaseproof paper and then in a double layer of foil and store in a cool place.

A day or two before Christmas wash the excess sugar from the angelica under water and pat dry with a cloth. Then cut out holly leaves if you can or just ordinary diamond leaf shapes. Cut a few glacé cherries in half. Then gently melt the redcurrant jelly in a pan and brush it all over the cake. Immediately arrange the angelica leaves and halved cherries in a pattern on top and sprinkle the sugar crystals all around. The crystals look like ice or frost and I also dot silver balls around the top and sides of the cake, which gives an added sparkle.

DARK CHOCOLATE CAKE

Serves 6–8

It has now become a tradition in our family to have this moist chocolate cake instead of the usual rich fruit cake at Christmas time. After the fruit-filled pudding and mince pies we all much prefer it and with its snowy-white frosting the appearance when decorated is perfectly seasonal.

For the cranberry and orange filling

4 fl oz (100 ml) fresh orange juice (about 2 oranges)
4 oz (100 g) sugar
8 oz (200 g) fresh cranberries

For the cake

4 oz (100 g) plain chocolate
3 tablespoons (3 × 15 ml spoon) water
6 oz (150 g) butter or margarine
10 oz (250 g) soft dark brown sugar
1 teaspoon (5 ml spoon) vanilla essence
3 large (size 4) eggs – lightly whisked
6 fl oz (150 ml) milk soured by adding the juice of ½ lemon
10 oz (250 g) plain flour
½ teaspoon (2.5 ml spoon) baking powder
1½ level teaspoons (3 × 2.5 ml spoon) bicarbonate of soda

For the frosting
2 large (size 4) egg whites

12 oz (300 g) caster sugar
good pinch of salt
juice of 1 lemon
½ tablespoon (15 ml spoon) water
½ teaspoon (2.5 ml spoon) cream of tartar
Christmas decorations

Make the filling first. Put the orange juice in a saucepan and stir in the sugar. Add the cranberries. Cover, bring to the boil and simmer for 5 minutes. Cool and chill well in the fridge before using.

Now line two greased 8½-9½ in. (22–24 cm) sandwich tins with greased greaseproof paper. Break the chocolate into small pieces, then put with the 3 spoons of hot water in a bowl over a pan of very hot water, stirring occasionally until smooth. Remove from the heat and cool slightly. Turn the oven to Gas Mark 4/350°F/180°C. Cream the fat with the sugar and vanilla essence until light and fluffy. Thoroughly beat in the eggs and melted chocolate. Add the soured milk alternately with the sifted flour, baking powder and bicarbonate of soda. Divide the mixture between the two tins and smooth with a knife. Bake towards the centre of the oven for 30–40 minutes until well risen and springy to touch in the centre. Leave in the tins for 10 minutes, then turn the cakes carefully out on to a wire tray to cool, and remove greaseproof paper. When cold, sandwich together with the cranberry and orange filling.

To make the frosting, put all the ingredients together in a large deep bowl and whisk together. Put the bowl over a pan of very hot water and continue to whisk for about 10 minutes until the mixture is thick enough to stand in peaks and the sugar has dissolved. Spread at once thickly all over the cake with a wide knife, making rough flicks, decorate, leave in a cool place but not the fridge.

You can, of course, make the cake in advance and freeze it. The icing is best done a day before you cut the cake.

BLACK BUN

Serves 8–10

In Scotland, as the clock strikes midnight on New Year's Eve, you cut your black bun and offer it around with a glass of whisky. It is a dark, succulent and concentrated mass of fruit, nuts and spices mixed with a lot of whisky, bound with very little flour and egg and sealed in a crisp pastry case. Needless to say, it is delicious and should be made weeks or months ahead to allow it to mature.

For the pastry
8 oz (200 g) plain flour
pinch of salt
4 oz (100 g) butter
egg yolk to glaze

For the filling
1 lb (400 g) currants
1 lb (400 g) raisins
2 oz (50 g) candied peel
4 oz (100 g) chopped or flaked blanched
   almonds
4 oz (100 g) plain flour
4 oz (100 g) soft brown sugar
1 teaspoon (5 ml spoon) each of ground
   cinnamon, ginger,
allspice or cloves and nutmeg
1 level teaspoon (5 ml spoon) cream of
   tartar

SEASONAL CAKES

1 level teaspoon (5 ml spoon)
  bicarbonate of soda
1 lightly whisked egg
8 tablespoons (8 × 15 ml spoon) whisky
3 level tablespoons (3 × 15 ml spoon)
  black treacle

Grease an 8 in. (20 cm) round cake tin. Make the pastry in the usual way. Leave to rest while you mix up the filling.

Mix all the dry ingredients for the filling together in a large bowl. Stir in the egg and whisky. Melt the treacle in a pan to make it runny and stir it in.

Roll out two-thirds of the pastry into a circle about 14 in. (35 cm) in diameter. Line the cake tin with it, making sure the pastry comes up above the top of the sides of the tin. Spoon the filling in and level it. Fold the top of the pastry over. Roll out the remaining pastry to an 8 in. (20 cm) circle – you can put the tin on the pastry and cut it round to make an even circle. Moisten the edges of the pastry, put on the circle lid and press the edges firmly together. I use leftover bits of pastry to decorate and to write "Happy New Year" in cut-out letters, which makes the glazed black bun look most impressive.

Lastly, with a skewer, make 4 or 5 holes right down to the bottom of the cake, then prick all over the top with a fork and brush with egg yolk. Bake in the centre of the oven at Gas Mark 4/350°F/ 180°C for 2½-3 hours. When the pastry turns a rich golden brown lay a piece of foil on top so it doesn't get any darker. Turn carefully out of the tin and cool. Store in an airtight tin or wrapped in foil in a cool place.

LEMON GINGER SHORTBREAD
Makes about 16

For many years we spent New Year with friends in Scotland. After the clock had struck twelve we used to wrap up and set out to first-foot in the few neighbouring cottages under the moor. At each cottage we were offered a piece of Black bun and some shortbread, which were often helped down with a home-brewed and extremely potent liqueur. In Scotland, it is traditional to have shortbread in the house to offer to friends throughout the festive season. You must hide this away in a tin or it will get eaten up too quickly! If you like you can use wholemeal flour which will give a nuttier taste and texture.

*8 oz (250 g) butter, plus extra for
    greasing\
4 oz (125 g) icing sugar
grated rind of 2 lemons
6 oz (175 g) plain flour
2 oz (50 g) cornflour
3 oz (75 g) ground rice
2 rounded teaspoons (2 x 5 ml spoons)
    ground ginger
caster sugar*

Put the butter, the icing sugar and the grated lemon rind into a bowl and cream them together with a whisk. This doesn't need to be done very thoroughly. Mix the flour, cornflour, ground rice and ginger together in a bowl and the gradually whisk them into the creamed butter and sugar. Using floured hands gather up the dough, divide it in half and press it quickly into two buttered 8-inch (20 cm) sandwich tins. Prick all over with a fork. Heat the oven to Gas Mark 2/300°F/150°C. Bake the shortbread on the bottom shelf for 60–70 minutes until it is a pale golden colour. Cut the shortbread into pieces in the tins while still hot. Sprinkle with caster sugar and leave until almost cold before carefully taking out with a spatula.

HONEYED APRICOT AND BRANDY CAKE

Serves 8–10

This cake has a light texture which makes a good contrast to the heavier Christmas foods. The flavour of honey and brandy is very distinct and the apricots give the cake a refreshing sharpness.

*8 oz (250 g) dried apricots
4 oz (125 g) seedless raisins
4 fl oz (125 ml) brandy
4 fl oz (125 ml) unsweetened fresh
    orange juice
6 oz (175 g) self-raising flour, plus extra
2 teaspoons (2 x 5 ml spoons) baking
    powder
6 oz (175 g) softened butter, plus extra
    for greasing
4 rounded tablespoons (4 x 15 ml
    rounded spoons) honey
4 medium–large eggs (size 2–3),
    separated
1 teaspoon (5 ml spoon) caraway seeds
icing sugar*

Chop up the dried apricots and put them in a saucepan with the raisins. Pour in the brandy and orange juice. Cover the pan and bring to the boil over a medium heat. Stir well, and them remove from the heat and leave on one side for at least an hour.

Thoroughly butter and flour a 8½–9-inch (21–25 cm) diameter, deep, loose-based cake tin. Sift the flour and baking powder into a bowl. Heat the oven to Gas Mark 4/350°F/180°C. Cream the butter with the honey until light and fluffy. Whisk in the egg yolks one at a time, whisking hard after each addition. Then, using a metal spoon, stir in half of the flour followed by the apricot and raisin mixture and the caraway seeds. Then stir in the rest of the flour. Lastly, whisk the egg whites until they stand in soft peaks and fold them gently into the cake mixture a bit at a time, using a large metal spoon. Spoon into the prepared tin and spread level.

Cook just below the centre of the oven for 60–70 minutes until a small knife comes out clean. Remove from the oven, leave in the tin for 10 minutes or more, and then push the cake out of the tin and manoeuvre it with a spatula on to a cooking rack. Before serving sprinkle a fairly thick layer of icing sugar through a sieve over the top of the cake.

FRUITED CHOCOLATE CHRISTMAS CAKE

Serves about 16

This is a real fruit cake but it is also a real chocolate cake. It is densely packed with dried pineapple, prunes, peel, raisins, crystallized ginger and walnuts: a mixture which combines irresistibly with the rich chocolate flavour. I make the cake two or three weeks before Christmas and then glaze if with apricot jam and ice it with lemony royal icing only two or three days before eating it, so that the icing is still slightly soft.

6 oz (175 g) dried pineapple pieces
6 oz (175 g) dark cooking chocolate
4 oz (125 g) unsalted butter, plus extra for greasing
5 oz (150 g) soft dark brown sugar
4 large eggs (size 1–2), beaten
5 oz (150 g) self-raising flour
2 tablespoons (2 x 15 ml spoons) cocoa
3 oz (75 g) ground almonds
5 tablespoons (5 x 15 ml spoons) brandy or rum
2 teaspoons (2 x 5 ml spoons) ground cinnamon
4 oz (125 g) soft pitted prunes, chopped roughly
4 oz (125 g) crystallized ginger, chopped roughly

COOKING FOR CHRISTMAS

4 oz (125 g) walnuts, chopped roughly
4 oz (125 g) candied peel
6 oz (175 g) raisins
coarsely grated rind of 2 lemons

Put the dried pineapple into a bowl, pour over plenty of boiling water and leave for 15–30 minutes and then drain. Line the base of a deep, 9-inch (23 cm) round cake tin with a piece of well buttered greaseproof paper. Line the sides with a wide strip of buttered paper which comes up above the edges of the tin.

Melt the chocolate in a bowl over hot water. Cream the butter and the brown sugar in a mixing bowl, add the melted chocolate and whisk thoroughly until smooth, paler in colour and fluffy. Add the beaten eggs a little at a time, whisking well after each addition. Then sift the flour and cocoa into the bowl and fold them in with a large metal spoon. Fold in the ground almonds, the brandy and the cinnamon. Then fold in the chopped prunes, ginger, walnuts, the candied peel, the raisins and the grated lemon rind. Lastly stir in the soaked pineapple pieces.

Spoon the mixture into the lined cake tin and level the top. Heat the oven to Gas Mark 3/325°F/170°C and bake the cake in the centre for one hour; then turn down to Gas Mark 1/275°F/140°C for 1¼–1½ hours until a knife stuck in the centre comes out clean. Leave the cake in the tin for 10–15 minutes and then take it out of the tin and leave it on a rack to cool. When cold, wrap well in several layers of cling film and store in a cool place until you are ready to ice it.

SEASONAL DRINKS

"Whene'er a bowl of punch we make,
Four striking opposites we take :
The strong, the weak, the sour, the sweet,
Together mixed most kindly meet:
And when they happily unite
The bowl is pregnant with delight."

In spite of this rhyme, which I found in an old cookery book, the word punch comes from the Indian word panch meaning five – i.e., five ingredients. However, there are all sorts of punches, with varying numbers of ingredients, and you may well have your own concoction. Their warm, spicy, potent taste is especially appropriate at Christmas time. Even those who usually dislike sweet things can enjoy a traditional, aromatic brew round the Christmas tree.

GLÜHWEIN

For about 6 people

This Austrian way of mulling wine is specially good for parties, as it has a nice fresh taste and transforms cheap wine.

1 large (1 litre) bottle cheap red wine
3–4 oz (75–100 g) sugar, to taste
1 teaspoon (5 ml spoon) whole cloves

1 teaspoon (5 ml spoon) ground
*   cinnamon*
juice of 1 orange and 1 lemon

Pour the wine into a saucepan. Add the other ingredients. Heat until nearly boiling, then strain into a warmed bowl and serve.

OLD-FASHIONED MULLED WINE
For about 6 people

A traditional recipe for a delicious, warming brew.

1 large (1 litre) bottle Spanish red wine
10 fl oz (250 ml) ginger ale or cold
*   strained tea*
1 orange, stuck with 10 cloves
3 cinnamon sticks or 1 teaspoon (5 ml
*   spoon) cinnamon powder*
2 teaspoons (2 × 5 ml spoon) mixed
*   spice*
4 oz (100 g) brown sugar
large wineglass of brandy or whisky or
*   dark rum*

Put all ingredients in a pan and heat thoroughly, without boiling, for about half an hour. Before serving add the brandy, whisky or rum.

CIDER PUNCH
For about 10 people

Here is a cheering punch which isn't too expensive.

2 pts (1 litre) sweet cider
1 teaspoon (5 ml spoon) each ground
*   cinnamon and nutmeg*
juice of 1 lemon

Put the ingredients in a pan, bring to the boil and simmer for about 5 minutes. Serve immediately.

NON-ALCOHOLIC PUNCH FOR CHILDREN'S PARTIES

For about 10 people

This refreshing, non-alcoholic punch is ideal for children's parties during the festive season – or at any time.

> 2 pts (1 litre) sugar syrup (1¼ pt (625 ml)
>   water and 12 oz (300 g) sugar)
> 2 pts (1 litre) water
> 1 pt (¼ litre) orange juice
> ½ pt (1 litre) grapefruit juice
> 1 teaspoon (5 g) each of ground ginger
>   and cinnamon
> 8 cloves
> mint and fruit to decorate, according to
>   season

Boil together for 5 minutes the sugar syrup, water and spices to extract the flavour. Add the orange and grapefruit juice and stir well. Serve either hot or chilled, decorated with mint and fruit, whatever is in season.

CHRISTMAS CHEER – A WASSAIL CUP

For about 10 people

If you have no personal concoction to warm the spirit at Christmas time and want to stick to old traditions, drink the health of your family and friends round the Wassail bowl on Christmas Eve or Twelfth Night. But remember to sing, too !

> 4 oz (100 g) sugar
> 3 cinnamon sticks or 2 teaspoons (2 ×
>   5 ml spoon) ground
> cinnamon
> ½ pt (250 ml) pineapple juice
> ½ pt (250 ml) orange juice
> juice of 2–3 lemons
> 5 fl oz (125 ml) dry sherry
> 2½-3 pts (1.25–1.5 litres) ale
> slices of lemon

Boil up the sugar, cinnamon and fruit juice together for 5 minutes. Pour the sherry and ale into a large pan and strain the fruit juice mixture into it. Heat but don't boil.

Garnish with slices of lemon and serve.

WHAT TO DRINK WITH WHAT

The rule about drink, as about food, is do what you like and try out new combinations. All that matters is that you please yourself and your family. Christmas is a time when most of us buy more drink than usual, and it is a special treat to serve a number of different wines with a meal. Christmas is one time you can do it without having expensive bottles left over, because you can as easily serve six people with a different bottle for each course, as three bottles of the same wine, which may go well with the turkey, but will taste a bit odd with the first courses, or the Christmas pudding. Here are a few ideas. I have just mentioned the type of wine I think goes well with each dish. Obviously, how good a wine you buy of each kind is a matter of choice.

WITH SNACKS, AUBERGINE PURÉE, ETC, OR FRIENDS WHO DROP IN

Apart from spirits and soft drinks (it is surprising how many people ask for cola or ginger beer) it is worth having Macon Blanc – dry and sharp. Serve well chilled. My favourite is the fragrant Chambery Vermouth, with ice and a slice of lemon. And, of course, sherry – Manzanilla, with its slightly salty taste, specially good with fish dishes or the smoky Aubergine Purée, or a Fino.

WITH THE TURKEY

Nothing can beat a good claret. It has the right weight for turkey – not so light that it gets lost, not so heavy that the turkey is outdone. For this reason I prefer it to Burgundy or Beaujolais. Some people prefer dry white wine or a Riesling or hock with turkey on the old-fashioned grounds that white wine and white meat go together. I think this is a mistake. Don't, whatever you do, forget to put the red wine in a warm room the night before and open it at least a couple of hours before drinking. The cheaper the red wine the more it benefits from being opened early to let the air get at it. Decanting it helps, too.

WITH THE CHRISTMAS PUDDING OR THE CHRISTMAS CAKE

Try not to go on drinking the red wine with the Christmas pudding. It is too sharp and can be too light. Christmas pudding is rich and needs a rich sweet wine to set it off. Buy a Sauternes or French sweet white wine, chill

SEASONAL DRINKS

well in the fridge for two or three hours and ou will be astonished how delicious it tastes even quite a cheap bottle. You could also y a rich Muscatel with the pudding, or even cream sherry, but save port for the nuts nd fruit at the end of the meal.

CHAMPAGNE OR SPARKLING WINE

is really worth buying a bottle or two of Champagne or one of the many sparkling vines now on the market. Just the sight f the bubbles and the pale golden colour heers up jaded spirits. You can drink it at ny time – before lunch, with the Christmas udding, at the end of the meal, when veryone feels rather full, or after the children ave been put to bed and you are in need of pick-me-up. It does not matter when you rink it, but to have it is to add a final touch ɔ the celebrations, and when you work out ie cost of a sparkling white wine, you will nd it is no more expensive than pouring gin nd tonic.

WITH COLD FOOD AND LEFTOVERS

have tried to suggest ways of making cold heat and salad different and enticing on Boxing Day and through the holiday. But if ou are going to take trouble with that, take rouble with the wine too. To drink the same wine you drank on Christmas Day is like serving leftovers.

Try a cold rosé – for instance, you may like the slightly sweet Rosé d'Anjou. Or chill a bottle of red wine – a Beaujolais does well. It tastes quite different from when it is warm – refreshing and brisk-tasting. A Côte du Rhône, with its slightly flinty taste, also goes well with cold meat. If you want a white wine a fresh Vouvray or a light dry white Spanish wine would do well. If your guests do not want to drink anything too heavy add soda water to the Spanish white wine, to make it light and sparkling.

Do try to remember to make sure the white wines are really cool. They lose a lot if they are served too warm. Don't be afraid to put a lump of ice in them if the worst comes to the worst – though it is better to find a container that can act as an ice bucket.

If you have anything left in your budget I would lay in a stock of beer and lager, and buy a small bottle of liqueur, perhaps cherry brandy, as a luxury to drink with your coffee. And a bottle of Perrier water, or another sparkling water, which served with a slice of lemon and ice looks, and is, healthy and restoring, particularly when you've eaten too much.

INDEX

Sauces

Apricot and Clementine sauce 15
Boxing day curried sauce for turkey 75
Bread sauce 12
Brown bread sauce 13
Chilled brandy sauce 21
Cucumber sauce 46
Lychee sauce 43
Onion, brandy and orange sauce 14
Rum butter 21
Spiced cranberry and orange sauce 14
Thyme and mustard sauce 52

Soup

Vegetable consommé with shredded
  lettuce 28
Walnut soup 29

Stuffing

Chestnut stuffing 10
Chestnut and parsnip stuffing 10
Gooseberry and brazil nut stuffing 36
Green herb stuffing 11
Raisin and rosemary stuffing 64
Veal, lemon and parsley stuffing 12

Turkey

Ravishing roulade 67
Roasting 8
Turkey au Gratin with Almonds 39

Veal

Country veal terrine 65
Veal, lemon and parsley stuffing 12
Walnut stuffed breast of veal 70

Walnuts

Celery and walnut pies 30
Cucumber, olive and walnut salad 73
Date and walnut mincemeat 78
Glossy fruit and walnut Christmas cake 89
Spiced pheasant with onions and walnuts 44
Walnut soup 28
Walnut stuffed breast of veal 70